The Life
and Times
of J. D. Sumner

The Life
and Times
of J. D. Sumner

THE WORLD'S LOWEST
BASS SINGER

An Updated, Expanded Version
of the Original Book,
Gospel Music Is My Life

J. D. SUMNER with **Bob Terrell**

Library of Congress Catalog Card Number: 94–090151

ISBN Number: 1-878894-04-8

Printed in the United States of America

TO MARY

For everything you meant to me,
and to my career as a singer.

Contents

Introduction
By James Blackwood

The story of J. D. Sumner's life is inspirational. It is not simply a rags-to-riches story, because he isn't that rich—in worldly goods, that is. He is tremendously rich in family, friends, a God-given ability to sing lower than anybody I ever heard, in having a fertile mind, and in the persuasive power to make others want to follow him and do the things he dreams up. J.D.'s story parallels, for the last half-century at least, the advancement of gospel music, and he has been right up there in the front all the way.

During the first twenty-five of his fifty years in gospel music, J. D. had a hand in most of the major developments within the industry: adoption of the bus as a mode of quartet travel, which was his sole idea; development of songwriting trends and publication of associated materials; recording innovations; perfection of sound equipment; quartet development; teaching others to sing; establishment of the National Quartet Convention, the Gospel Music Association, and the Dove Awards for excellence in gospel singing. You name it, he's had a hand in it.

J. D. sang with the Blackwood Brothers, whom I managed, for eleven years, and he and I worked together in gospel music for many, many more years. He is like a brother to me.

I met J. D. when he was with the Sunshine Boys working out of Wheeling, West Virginia. They came South and we worked some all-night sings together.

Soon after that, the Blackwood Brothers had an airplane crash in Clanton, Alabama, that took the lives of our baritone, R. W. Blackwood, and our bass, Bill Lyles. It all but destroyed the Blackwood Brothers Quartet. My first thoughts were to quit. In fact, as I came back to Memphis that night in the Statesmen car, I said I would never sing again, that I was finished. That was my sincere feeling.

The feeling didn't last long because singing was my life. The crash was on Wednesday, June 30, 1954; the funeral service was on Friday; and the following Monday, Bill Shaw, Jackie Marshall, and I—the remaining members of the quartet—drove to Fort Worth, Texas, and went on stage and sang.

I really don't remember much about that singing. We might have sung one song that night or we might have sung twenty. I just remember going there and going on stage. For some time, I was in a state of shock, and I don't remember a lot of things clearly about those days.

One thing I do remember was while I was emerging from shock, I began to think about replacements for Bill and R. W. I didn't have to look far to find R. W.'s replacement on the baritone. His brother, Cecil, was ready, and we made that decision pretty fast. But finding a bass presented a greater problem.

One bass singer, George Younce, told me later, or I heard later, that he came to Memphis to audition. I don't even remember that, but I'm sure he did.

I am also sure that God was directing my thoughts during those days because no one could have been farther from being a singer like Bill Lyles than J. D. Sumner. If it had been imperative to replace Bill with someone who could help keep our sound the way it had been, I certainly wouldn't have chosen J. D. Sumner.

But I called only one other person about the job. We discussed it and he would have accepted, but I backed out. Again I feel this was God directing me, because I then called J. D.

Our quartet and the Sunshine Boys had not been close; we didn't even know each other very well. But J. D. accepted the job and I was immediately satisfied that we had hired the right man. I felt it was meant to be. I still feel that way.

J. D. came with us the first of August 1954, and among our first thoughts was to decide on a means of transportation. We had been flying to all our engagements for two and a half years, but we immediately gave up the idea of flying again and bought a seven-passenger car like most other quartets used.

For a long time I had managed the quartet and was accustomed to doing about everything myself. I always felt I'd rather do something than to ask somebody else to do it. So, the first few weeks J. D. was with us, I loaded the records and P. A. system into the trailer, drove the quartet to the concert, unloaded the records and P. A. system, set them up, and after we finished singing, I'd reload all this stuff and drive wherever we were going next.

This went on for a little while and one day J. D. came to me and said, "I don't want to butt in, but do you really want to keep doing all this by yourself?"

I said, "Well, no, not really, but. . . ."

"All right, then," he said, "let me do some of it."

Starting there, J. D. began to take an awful lot off my shoulders.

One day, Jackie Marshall complained because J. D. told him to do something, so J. D. said, "Okay, we'll all divide the jobs."

With my permission, he assigned certain chores to each man. When he put Jackie and Bill Shaw in charge of records, Bill collared Jackie and said, "Now you've done it. We had it pretty easy, but now you've got us jobs."

It wasn't long afterward that J. D. came up with the idea of buying a bus to travel in. We had a lot of fun kidding him about a bus, but he kept at us until he sold us on the idea and we bought one. Then all the other quartets had a good time kidding us. Wasn't practical, they said; it would never work. I remember Jake Hess was one of those who ribbed J. D. the most about the bus, but they were always ribbing each other anyhow. Yet when J. D. convinced Jake one night that bus-riding was comfortable, Jake talked Hovie Lister into buying a bus for the Statesmen.

Now all gospel singers and most country and western and rock artists travel in their own private customized buses, and J. D. Sumner started it all with that first bus of ours back in 1955. There are hundreds, maybe thousands of buses on the road in the United States right now, hauling singers and entertainers all over the land.

For many years J. D. was one of the most productive song

writers in gospel music. When he came with us, he had written two songs. One was *When I'm Alone,* which became a popular song for us, and the other, which we never did record, nor did anyone else, was *Working in the Sawmill for Jesus.* It didn't quite make the hit charts.

While some of the groups were having fun with J. D. about his song, I saw that he had a great potential and encouraged him to write songs. About all it would take was a suggestion and the next day, or sometimes even an hour or two later, he would come around with the song.

We recorded practically everything J. D. wrote for a long time—his songwriting was that good.

Unfortunately, J. D. doesn't write songs now, not like he did. He's too busy. He wrote practically all of his songs when he was singing with us.

We were a happy quartet, and very successful, as the Blackwood Brothers had been for many years. For eleven years after J. D. joined us, we made no changes in the singing parts of our quartet: Bill Shaw, Cecil, J. D., and me.

But change is inevitable, and it finally came to us.

We bought the Stamps Quartet Music Company and inherited the Stamps Quartet with it. The quartet had just about quit singing, but the name of the Stamps Quartet was famous and we thought it should be reorganized on a professional basis.

Again J. D. took charge. He picked five men to make up the new Stamps Quartet. He was in charge, he did their booking and overseeing while still singing with the Blackwood Brothers.

After a year or so, we became convinced that the man who ran the quartet should be a member of it, and J. D. came to me with the idea of switching over to sing bass for the Stamps Quartet and bringing Big John Hall from the Stamps to take over his bass part with the Blackwood Brothers.

I wasn't receptive to the idea because I had come to lean so heavily on J. D. But soon I saw that this would be the salvation of the Stamps Quartet, and I reluctantly agreed.

In the next few years, J. D. performed the most fantastic job of building a top-notch gospel quartet that has ever been accomplished in that length of time. He took a bunch of kids like Tony Brown, Duke Dumas, Donnie Sumner, and my sons,

Jimmy and Billy, and built a quartet that was in as great demand as any in the business. Their success was practically all due to J. D.'s efforts.

J. D. has the kind of personality that makes people accept him for what he is. He will say exactly what he thinks and how he feels. There is no put-on about him. Being able to communicate with people is one of the most important aspects of our business and if anyone can do that, it's J. D. Sumner. He can say things on stage that no one else in the business can get away with saying, and people love him for it. He is perfectly honest and frank, and people believe in him. That, I think, is largely responsible for his tremendous success.

I appreciate his honesty. J. D. and I have had a lot of joint enterprises; everything that I was a part of, J. D. had a hand in, and vice versa. I would trust him with anything I own, even my life. There is nothing in the world I wouldn't do for him, and I know he feels the same about me. I appreciate knowing someone like J. D. Sumner whom I can trust absolutely. This kind of mutual love, trust, and respect is too rare among mankind today.

As proof of my trust of him, my only two children, James, Jr., and Billy, were both in the Stamps Quartet under J. D.'s care for several years. Billy was only fourteen when he started playing drums for J. D. and many people questioned my judgment in letting a son so young go off with a group full time. But, of course, I wouldn't have let Billy go with just any group. I let him go with J. D. because J. D. would do for him the same as he would do for his own. He did that for all the kids in the Stamps Quartet.

J. D.'s contributions to gospel music are endless. At his suggestion, the Blackwood Brothers underwrote the first National Quartet Convention in Memphis in 1956, and it has grown to tremendous proportions. The Blackwood Brothers, again with J. D.'s help, obtained the charter for the Gospel Music Association from the State of Tennessee. We paid for the charter, all the legal fees connected with securing it and setting the GMA in motion, and we were happy to do so because we felt it was something that gospel music needed.

J. D. spent hundreds of hours working with the GMA without monetary compensation because he thought it was necessary for the growth of the industry. We put considerable money into singing schools in all parts of the country in an effort to get more young people interested. Gospel music gave us a livelihood for many years and we felt we owed it something in return. This was our way.

I know sincerely that J. D. Sumner's prime aim and goal all those years was to promote gospel music, and his was not a selfish goal. He wanted only to make the industry bigger and better.

That's the way with J. D. Sumner; he's completely honest all the way.

JAMES BLACKWOOD
Memphis, Tennessee

Foreword

Strange as it may sound, I knew J. D. Sumner several years before I actually met him. I knew him from the distance of my favorite seat in the balcony of the old Asheville City Auditorium. The night that J. D. and the Sunshine Boys literally tore up the Statesmen, of which you will read in the ensuing pages, I was there.

Thus, when J. D. went with the Blackwood Brothers as a replacement for the late Bill Lyles, I applauded the move as one that would make that version of the Blackwood Brothers one of the greatest quartets the world had ever known.

J. D.'s rise to prominence was not overnight. It was not a sudden thing. He found no ready-made stardom, no one waiting with open arms to welcome him to the stage. What he attained, he earned by the sweat of his brow and the depth of his voice. There is no harder worker, no more dedicated man in any trade or profession than J. D. Sumner.

This is his story. It is the narrative of a man possessed with a rare talent who grasped himself by the bootstraps and pulled himself and his family upward into a better, more rewarding life, and, in doing so, managed to help lift an entire industry—that of professional gospel singing—to national prominence, a state of bliss that, unfortunately, the industry has since managed to shoot down in flames.

Of the thirty books I have written, this was the first, and certainly the most pleasurable. In forty-eight years as a journalist, I have interviewed thousands of people, but never have I interviewed one who was as easy a subject as J. D. Sumner. The man had an uncanny knack for knowing exactly what I wanted of him, and he said it fluently and quickly into a tape recorder. In his own fashion, he let the chips fall where they may. That's the only way J. D. can be.

The original book, entitled *J. D. Sumner: Gospel Music Is My Life*, was written in 1970 and '71 and published by the John T. Benson Publishing Co. of Nashville, Tennessee, in October of 1971. The first press run produced 3,000 copies, many of which were sold at the National Quartet Convention that year where the book originally went on sale.

Unfortunately, when that printing was sold out, the book was never reprinted. J. D. and the Bensons came to odds over the Stamps Quartet's recording contract, which J. D. pulled away from Benson's Heart Warming label and placed with another company—and the book was never reprinted.

It lay in limbo for years, with hundreds of gospel music lovers demanding copies of it. After many years, J. D. managed to obtain the copyright, and he and I began to bring it up to date, filling in the gap between the time the book was published and today, a matter of twenty-two years or more, during which J. D. continued his amazing accomplishments in the entertainment industry.

It is said that a book is not written, that it is rewritten, and we can vouch for the truth of that statement. We have rewritten this book a dozen times over the years, tearing it apart and putting it back together again; so the book is the culmination of twenty-four years of work. We wrote until we reached the point that we were both satisfied with the book's content. Then we put it to press.

We hope you will enjoy reading it as much as we enjoyed writing it.

A final word: You may notice that in this book we merely skimmed the surface of the Stamps Quartet's six years of singing backup for Elvis Presley. The reason for that is that we summed up those years in a companion volume entitled *ELVIS: His Love for Gospel Music and J. D. Sumner*. We saw no need to repeat the content of that book in this one. The Elvis book ($10, plus $2 handling and mailing) is available to readers simply by contacting either J. D. or me.

BOB TERRELL
P.O. Box 66
Asheville, NC 28802

CHAPTER ONE

A Problem Solved

The year 1967 was a fine one all around for the Stamps Quartet, though for a couple of weeks there was some doubt it would turn out that way.

To begin with, we bought a new bus. It was our first new bus since the quartet was reorganized in 1964 and put on the road as a professional gospel group. We had been riding in a hot old bus that had no air-conditioning, and suddenly we found ourselves in high cotton.

We were excited. Inside, the bus wasn't finished yet—it wasn't partitioned and therefore was pretty noisy—but it was still like the Queen Mary in comparison with the old clunker we'd been riding.

Most of the fellows in the quartet were just kids then and were given to hollering and screaming and cutting up to celebrate our new good fortune. They were so happy they'd stay up half the night yelling and carrying on.

We were a happy group and we sang a lot. Traveling down the road, we would burst into song and run through a few numbers any time someone felt like it.

I suppose I joined in as much as anyone, and it didn't help my vocal cords—they had taken a beating over the last twenty-five years of singing bass as low as I could.

My throat hurt periodically and I began to suspect that I had problems, but I had no idea what was wrong. I was doing all the master-of-ceremonies work for the quartet, and in operating my other business ventures, I had to talk a lot on the telephone. Then, of course, there was the singing which added to, or maybe even created, the stress.

We were in Oklahoma City for a singing engagement when my voice grew weak and my throat began to hurt like blue blazes. I went to a doctor who diagnosed my trouble as polyps on the vocal cords and gave me a solemn warning: There was a good possibility that the growths were malignant.

"To put it mildly," he said, "you have some problems."

From there we went to Waxahachie, Texas, where we were running the Stamps Quartet School of Music, and I telephoned Betty Brewster, wife of the Blackwood Brothers' bus driver, Bundy Brewster, in Memphis. Betty worked for an eye, ear, nose, and throat doctor who recommended a doctor in Memphis who should do the operation to remove the polyps.

I flew to Memphis and had the doctor examine my throat. He didn't mince any words.

"You may have cancer of the vocal cords," he said flatly. He recommended an immediate removal of the polyps and told me it would be four days following the operation before he would know whether they were malignant. Medicine in 1967 wasn't what it is today; you could get an answer on malignancy the same day now.

I checked into the hospital that afternoon, eager to get the surgery over with and certainly dreading the results. I am not a fatalist and I knew that a lot of people were praying for me, which was a comfort.

I left the hospital three hours after I came out of the anesthesia. The doctor didn't especially want me to go, but I insisted and he relented. I wanted to get back to Texas and surround myself with those I knew and loved. I felt that was where I wanted to be when I got the news that would tell me if my singing career—perhaps even my life—was drawing to a close.

Before I left, the doctor told me that I could not say a word for two weeks—not one word. He was unyielding on that point.

So my wife, Mary, and I got in the car and headed for Texas. She had driven over from our home in Nashville to be with me during the operation. I was as relaxed as anybody can be who can't talk. I had no idea what the future held, or in fact, whether there would even be a future.

We arrived in Waxahachie and while I was among friends, a pall nevertheless descended over all of us.

Nobody will ever know what I went through those next four days.

And nobody will ever know how I felt when I had Mary call the doctor in Memphis at 11 o'clock on the morning of the fourth day following the operation.

I watched her face closely when she asked if the polyps were malignant and, of course, I could tell immediately when she began to smile as the doctor answered her.

I knew I didn't have cancer of the throat, and, brother, that's how you spell relief.

I felt so good about it that I went with the quartet on the road, although I couldn't open my mouth to sing a song or say a word.

Instead of talking, I wrote notes to the boys. I also carried a piece of paper on which I had written that I had had throat surgery and couldn't talk. When people approached me to talk, I showed them the paper.

It is hard not to be able to sing when singing is your life and you have lived it for so many years, but my relief was so great that I didn't have any trouble keeping my mouth shut.

I think the song that touched me most during those two weeks was *Now I Have Everything*, for I felt that now I did have everything.

There were a lot of happy people—and I suppose I was the happiest—when I finally stood on the stage of the War Memorial Auditorium in Nashville and broke two weeks of silence (a strange two weeks for me) by singing *Now I Have Everything*.

Singing that one song provided the greatest thrill of my life up to that moment.

For me, it heralded the continuation of a singing career that I had begun so many years ago in Florida and which Mary and I had clung to through thick and thin.

Much of the time, especially in the early years, things were usually thin.

The thick came later, after a lot of sacrifice and hard work.

In the years since that throat operation I have accomplished two things of which I am extremely proud. First, through sheer hard work and enough luck to find the right people at the right time, I have built the Stamps Quartet into what many people consider to be the finest male quartet in the world today. And secondly, the Stamps Quartet and I logged six years singing backup with the world's greatest entertainer, Elvis Presley. For the last six years of his life, he never went on stage without the Stamps Quartet to sing with him.

This is my story.

CHAPTER TWO

A Kid in Lakeland

When I was a kid in Lakeland, Florida, where I was born November 19, 1924, and christened John Daniel Sumner, I never heard the word "poverty" used. We were poor as church mice but never for a moment did we consider ourselves poverty-stricken or destitute. Most of our friends and neighbors were in the same fix, but we all simply worked a little harder trying to improve our lot.

My father was John S. Sumner. He died in 1965. My mother was Lelia Sumner, who lived on in Lakeland in an apartment house that I owned. Her maiden name was Lelia Lee. She was a direct descendant of Robert E. Lee. She lived to the age of ninety and died in 1987.

The town of Lakeland was not very large when I came along, and we lived there about half the time. My father farmed in the summer and in the winter worked in the fruit groves, picking oranges and lemons. We would move back and forth from town, where we spent the winters, to some land he rented in the country to grow vegetables in the summer. As far back as I can remember, I helped him in the harvest. I picked the lower branches of the trees while he picked the high ones.

Our house in the country was built on stilts and it was pretty high. We had a front porch, and a big back porch where we had a pump. The well was under the back porch. Our stove was a big iron wood range upon which my mother did the cooking and canning and heated water every Saturday, just as faithfully as Saturday came, for each of us to take our baths. Nobody took a bath except on Saturday.

Mama heated water on the stove, poured it into a wash tub on the back porch, pumped in enough cold water to temper it, and we'd take a bath right there on the porch. We didn't have to worry about privacy. We lived so far in the country nobody ever walked up on us.

We were at our place in the country when the first hurricane that I can remember hit us. I was about five years old; it was just before I started to school.

For two or three days it rained like the sky was falling, but that was only the forerunner of the hurricane itself. When the big blow hit, our house rocked so hard that we feared it would fall off the stilts.

My father lined us up according to our ages, facing the front door. I was first because I was the baby. My sister Myrtis was next. Then came my brother Russell, whom we call Buddy, and then Bernice, the oldest. Mother got in line after Bernice, and Dad brought up the rear.

He cautioned us to stay in line and if the house started to go over and he gave the word, we were to run out to the strawberry shed and take cover. We stayed lined up like that all night while the hurricane raged and the house shook, but, thank the Lord, Dad didn't have to sound the charge.

*   *   *

My dad could neither read nor write. He only went to school a short time. Today, when education means so much, he would probably be judged pretty dumb. But literacy wasn't everything then. My dad was smart as a whip in other areas—like counting money.

Money was tight. It had to be conserved, even pinched. My father knew exactly how much money we could afford to spend at any given time, and he knew the prices of everything we might need to buy at the store. It was necessary that men know these things.

When my mother and dad got ready to go to the store to make their weekly purchases, she would sit down and call off the list of things she needed, like a box of matches, five pounds of sugar, ten pounds of potatoes, two pounds of lard. She never called off eggs because we had our own chickens.

My father would listen to the items she named and we could see his lips move slightly as he counted, and the moment my mother finished calling off the list, my father would have the bill figured in his head.

He might say, "That comes to five dollars and eighty cents. You must whittle it down. Take something out. Get a pound of lard instead of two, or get four pounds of sugar."

During the summer when my father farmed, he didn't make any money. Our rich time was in the winter when he worked in the fruit. That's when he made his money. He got so he would buy a hundred pounds of sugar, maybe twenty pounds of flour, ten pounds of corn meal, things like that in large quantity, and would store all this up for the summer when we didn't make any money. There were times before he started doing this that we darned near starved to death.

*   *   *

My father came by his frugality the hard way. He learned it early in life, really, but lost touch with penny-pinching for a while after he got married. Then the depression came along and put him right back where he had been before.

When he was a kid money was even tighter than it was when I was a boy. The only money my dad ever got was a nickel at Christmas. His sisters got a dime. One of his sisters, Aunt Lou, always wanted to trade her dime for his nickel because the nickel was bigger. Dad was smart enough to make the deal; he knew he could cash in that jewel at the store and have himself two nickels instead of one.

There was the usual amount of happiness and tragedy in my father's boyhood. Once his mother and father went out and left the kids in the charge of their oldest son, my Uncle Bob. The smaller kids played around the house while Uncle Bob worked in the field. The youngest was Grover, who was four. The other children built a large fire and dared Grover to run through it. He didn't know any better and backed off and tried to dash through but lost his breath in the midst of it, inhaled the flames, and died.

My granddaddy was a rather wealthy man for the time and place. He owned 7,000 acres of land near Live Oak, Florida, and had a fence all the way around his property. Every Sunday after church and a big family dinner, my father and his brothers and sisters had to pull the grass from around this fence. That in itself was a pretty tall chore, but they could keep up with it by applying themselves every Sunday after-noon.

Through the week they farmed. That's why my father quit school early: to help with the farming. He and his larger brothers plowed two-mule teams, and the girls plowed with one mule.

Times were hard then, not only financially but in all other ways, too. Illnesses that we would dose into oblivion today with all the medications we have, used to kill people. Appendicitis was a killer. They didn't have much medicine of any kind, and any time a pain hit somebody in the stomach he grabbed the castor oil. Epidemics of influenza wiped out half the population.

I have heard my father say that my granddaddy spent his fortune trying to save one of his eyes.

When my dad and his brothers got married, my grand-daddy gave each of them 1,500 acres of land and a newly-built log cabin as a wedding present. They were then on their own.

Granddaddy died at the age of fifty-six and dad sold his own property in Live Oak and moved to Lakeland. He leased the Palms Hotel and operated it till it was condemned.

The condemnation came about in an odd way. The man who owned the hotel saw my father was making good money with it, and he wanted it back. The plumbing in the hotel was pretty bad, so he went to Tallahassee to pull some political strings and get the hotel condemned because of the plumbing. He intended to get my daddy out of it, do some work on the plumbing, and reopen the hotel himself.

But he didn't reckon with my daddy's temper. Dad went to Tallahassee, too, and by the time both of them got through there, they made the owner tear the cotton-picking hotel down—right to the ground.

Out of the hotel business then, my dad bought three big houses, turned them into rooming houses and ran them till the depression came and he lost everything.

That's when we started having it rough. Until then, I suppose I was a pretty rich kid.

*   *   *

I always had a lot of pride. About 1931, at the depth of the depression, we had to become "mossers" just to exist. We pulled Spanish moss out of trees in the country and sold it at a moss factory, making about nine dollars a week. My dad, my brother Russell, and I gathered so much moss—and I am sure others did the same—that soon there was none left within easy reach, except in town. So we began to work the town and in addition to what we were paid at the moss factory, we were making about fifty cents off each family that hired us to pull their moss.

We were gathering moss one day in the yard of my school teacher, Mrs. Joseph Swan, and she asked my father to send me into the house for a sandwich and Coke. A Coke was really a treat then and I enjoyed it, but that's the most embarrassed I ever was—to know that my teacher knew we were so poor we had to gather moss for a living.

*   *   *

Transportation was something else in those days. We had a car, such as it was, and the main trips we made were to church and back, six or eight miles each way. There was nothing uncommon about having three or four flat tires on a trip to church. We fixed them by taking one tire and cutting "boots" from it to cover the holes in the blown tire.

Once a year we went to camp meeting in Wimauma, Florida, a trip of forty-five miles each way, and you can't imagine the preparation we had to go through just to get the car ready for the trip. It had to go to the garage for a thorough check-over, and we had to get the best tires we could muster without buying anything. We weren't able to buy tires so we just had to make do the best way we could. It was nothing for us to have fifteen flats on the forty-five mile trip.

Camp meetings lasted all day and far into the night—and went on for ten days. Usually we had a little money to spend for fun. During the winter while my father worked in the fruit to make what little money we needed for staples, my mother worked in the canning factory in Lakeland and gave each of us children a nickel a week for doing chores around the house. Mine were washing dishes and raking the yard on Saturdays. I saved all winter and when springtime—and camp meeting—rolled around, I would have a dollar or a dollar and a half.

At camp meeting I rationed my money. If I had a dollar, I could spend a dime a day. If I had been fortunate enough to save a dollar-fifty, I could spend fifteen cents a day. At those dollar-and-a-half camp meetings, I bought a nickel ice cream cone at 11 o'clock in the morning, another at 4 in the afternoon, and either a third ice cream cone or a nickel glass of lemonade after the service at night.

There were five services a day at camp meeting, and this is where I was introduced to gospel quartet singing.

Camp meetings looked like tent cities. Most people lived in tents that they made themselves by stretching wire from tree to tree or pole to pole (if all the trees were taken) and pegging their canvas, or whatever they used for a tent, across the wire and to the ground on either side. They draped blankets on the inside to divide one sleeping area from another. Everybody cooked on open fires outside their tents. Sleeping was accomplished however a family preferred, or could afford. Some were fortunate enough to have cots, many of the World War I variety. I slept on the ground, quite comfortably, too, for camp meeting was an Occasion with a capital "O."

The music at camp meeting was gospel, of course, not nearly as refined as it is now and certainly in no way as commercial. The singing was great, though. Such groups as the LeFevre Trio and the Homeland Harmony Quartet came to our camp meetings and while they were terrific for the times, their sound could not compare with the electronic sounds of today's gospel music.

I am sure it was at camp meeting that I got my first encouragement to become a singer.

Our pastor was the Rev. I. H. Marks. His daughter, Naomi, married Frank Stamps, one of the early giants and founders of the gospel music profession. They used to attend camp meetings and Mr. Stamps would sing.

What a fine bass voice he had! I'll never forget the day he sang *Stand By Me*. He had no public address set, just the power of his vocal cords, and what a wonderful job he did on that song! About five thousand people were there. I was in the back and could hear every word Mr. Stamps sang as well as if I had been on the front row.

*   *   *

My father was a smoker. He smoked cigarettes, but we were so poor he didn't always have money to buy them—or even to buy a sack of Bull Durham. That's when I really came in handy. He would send me out on the street to shoot butts— to pick up cigarette butts that he would tear apart, throwing away the paper and that part of the tobacco that had been in the smoker's mouth, and pouring the rest of the tobacco into a pile on a piece of paper. When the pile got large enough— after I had shot enough butts—he would reroll the tobacco into cigarettes of his own.

Many people today believe smoking is a sin. It wasn't judged in that sense back then. About ninety-nine percent of grown men smoked and that was that. My father really liked his cigarettes.

We had family prayer every night and morning at our house, and it was at one of these sessions that my butt-shooting led my father to grief.

We had no electricity in our home. Our lights were kerosene lamps and during the evening family prayer it was my job, being the youngest, to sit in my mother's lap and hold the lamp so she could see to read the Bible.

She would read a chapter and then make each of us pray, starting with me and proceeding through the ranks according to age . . . Myrtis, Buddy, Bernice, and then Daddy. About forty percent of the time Daddy was not in a praying mood, but she made him pray anyway and he would never pray so you could understand him. He would mumble, "Brmph, blgerum, woreeh . . . amen!" He'd get through his prayer in record time.

On one of these nightly prayer occasions, I had misfigured on my butt-shooting time and had gone out looking too close to prayer time. In addition to that mistake, I had also fogged up one of the butts and taken a few puffs for myself. The odor of tobacco was still on my breath as I crawled up into my mother's lap to hold the lamp, and when I looked into her face and smiled, she caught a whiff of my breath—and it curled her hair.

Talk about an old man getting chewed out, my father did! I escaped scot free, Mother was so intent on making certain that he didn't send me out shooting butts any more.

CHAPTER THREE

School Days and the Town Bully

Kids have all sorts of problems now with school-days marked by heavy enrollment, drugs, and peer pressure. We had problems, too, though nothing like this. But problems are problems when you are young and in school, and the smallest problem can be severe to a youngster.

Our problems were bullies. We had these big bullies in school who would wear you out if you got the least bit out of line. . . .

I got my education in a number of places and at one time walked five miles to school barefoot. In the morning I rolled out of bed at daylight, did my chores, like putting the mule out to pasture and getting the cow out—my dad did the milking until I got to be an older boy—and then I'd take off to school.

I had no shoes because we got only one pair a year and either wore them out pretty fast or saved them for Sundays.

In the wintertime many mornings are frosty in Florida and walking barefoot through five miles of frost can cool your feet considerably.

When in Lakeland we lived in a small house on Fifth Street and attended school nearby. My brother Buddy was the biggest boy in school and as long as he went to school I had no problems; I could whip up on the kids without interference because Buddy would be standing by.

But when Buddy left school, I began to get my come-uppance. I had been the bully until then because he'd take up for me, but the tables turned and I was the bully no longer.

For almost two years, I could look forward to getting a

whipping every morning at recess and another at noon. Those other bullies had themselves a time.

Finally, I decided I would either have to start defending myself or be turned into a solid lump. I chose to take my stand, put up my dukes, and began to square things off. Times changed after that.

I had a cousin named Herbert Sumner who was two years older than I. The year he was thirteen and I was eleven we decided we had gotten all the home life we could put up with, and for some time we planned to run away. A lot of kids bugged out back then, many, many more than do today. Families were larger and kids ran away to make things easier on their parents.

Herbert and I talked about all the reasons for running away that we could think of and came to the conclusion that it was the right thing to do. All we needed, I suppose, was an excuse that would build our nerve.

This excuse came along one afternoon as we walked home from school.

We got to the railroad tracks and there stood this big bully who could mop up on about anybody he wanted to. He stood there blocking our path and we knew that one of us, and possibly both, had had it.

I looked quickly around for a weapon and saw a railroad spike that had been dropped by section hands who'd been replacing crossties. I grabbed the spike and Herbert and I both jumped this bully.

Some way I laid that railroad spike alongside his temple, and then held it there, threatening mayhem, while Herbert whipped him—and he *did* put a whipping on him. Herbert beat that bully until he passed out, and I held the spike to his temple so he didn't dare move while Herbert let him have it.

We didn't have much compassion for this bully; he'd been beating us up regularly at school and had threatened to tear us up right there at the railroad tracks.

That was the excuse we needed. We thought we'd killed him, so instead of facing up to the consequences, we lit out, straight down the railroad tracks as we'd been planning to do anyway.

We didn't even go home, but headed east along the rails toward Orlando, sixty-five miles away, where I had an uncle who was a paint contractor. We thought we'd go up there and work for him.

We did all right until darkness settled in. Then the surroundings became strange—and an eleven-year-old boy can see a lot of spooks in the dark. But we continued toward Orlando, making good time.

About 9:30, however, I was worn out. It was wintertime and the air became chilly. Soon I sat down on the rail and began to cry. I wouldn't go any farther.

That threw Herbert into a quandary. He didn't want to go on alone in the dark, and he knew what would be waiting if he turned back, but that was his final decision: He headed for home, and I followed him.

We got home after midnight and went to my house first, but were scared to go inside. From where I sat under a window, I could hear my mother crying. They had checked with the police and every other agency they could think of and nobody had seen or heard of us. You'd better believe that bully wasn't talking, not after what had happened to him.

Finally, when I heard my mother sob that she knew I was dead, I could stand it no longer. Like the common criminal I felt I was, I went inside and gave myself up.

My mother grabbed me and was so glad to see me that I didn't get a whipping, but Herbert wasn't so fortunate. When he got home, he evermore got the slat.

*   *   *

I went to Lakeland Junior High for the seventh grade, then to Griffin, about six miles out of Lakeland, for the eighth. My parents were always moving back and forth, remember, because my father wanted to live in the country and be a farmer and my mother wanted to live in town.

By then I was growing tall and in my eighth year in school I was a pretty good basketball player. I was captain of our team and scored more points that year by almost eighty than all the rest of the members of the team put together. I jumped center and then switched to forward where I could score more.

I graduated from Griffin, which only went through the eighth grade, then started to Kathleen High School. Kathleen was about five miles on out in the country and I was fifteen years old when I started the ninth grade.

I had learned to drive the car when I was eleven, and that was my undoing when it came to schooling. That was the year my brother Buddy got married when he was sixteen, so I began to take the car out at night and gradually began to date the girls. My daddy let me drive the car any time I wanted to. Not many boys get to take the family car and go dating when they're eleven.

Whether learning to drive at that early age was responsible for my own early marriage—also at the age of sixteen—is problematical, but it darned sure is the reason I dropped out of school after the eighth grade.

Our family still had a financial problem. We were always poor, but my daddy was a hard worker and one thing he did was trade cars every year. Times were hard but he just believed in working his way out of the hole and we were never without a car, even during the depression. He didn't trade for new cars, of course, just cars that would provide us with transportation.

And when we got hold of sixteen cents for a gallon of gas, we were in business.

*   *   *

I enrolled at Kathleen for the ninth grade and got mixed in with three boys who had a little money and not much desire for academics.

My father had a 1925 Hudson, a great big job that he let me drive to school, but instead of staying in school the four of us would drive over to St. Petersburg and spend the day at the beach.

This was a lot more fun than sitting in class, and it was only sixty miles.

We went to the beach every school day for four months and when time came to bring report cards home, I made up a story that the cards weren't ready and convinced my father.

We ran a pretty tight schedule, arriving home each day about the same time the other kids were getting home from school. Not any of our close neighbors had kids in the same grade with me, so I was safe there.

I told my father some good stories about what I was learning—and I was learning some things, but not from school books.

A water pump broke up our beachcombing and changed the course of my life. We had no city water out in the country and everyone depended on wells for water, even the schools. Some who were better off than others had electric or gasoline pumps but mostly the pumps were manually operated.

I picked up the boys at the regular time one day and drove to St. Pete where we spent the usual time lollygagging on the beach.

Back at school, meanwhile, the water pump broke down soon after school began, and the principal dismissed classes at 10 in the morning and sent all the kids home.

At the regular time, I drove home, stopping at a country store near our house where a lot of people usually hung out. My father was waiting for me there. He knew I had been playing hookey.

"Where have you been?" he asked.

"Where do you think I've been?" I asked in reply, like the smart aleck I was becoming. "I've been to school where I always go."

"What time did you get out?" he asked, keeping his cool.

"Well, isn't that stupid?" I said. "What time do you think I got out? I got out at three o'clock."

"That's amazing." He furrowed his brow. "Truly amazing. The rest of the children got out at ten o'clock this morning when the water pump broke, and they kept you there till three."

Right then, I knew I had a problem.

He took me behind the store where they threw these five-gallon lard cans when they emptied them. He bent double the lid of one of those cans and put my head between his knees, the way he'd found it best to hold me, and began to work on me. When he locked those bony knees right back of my ears, I couldn't move, and that day he made good use of that fact. He wore out four lard can lids on me and I thought he was going to kill me.

I survived, however, but my beachcombing days were done. He made me quit school and put me to work in the fields, hoeing beans and pulling fodder in the summer. If you have ever pulled fodder, you know what sort of job it is, the way it scratches your arms and makes you itch all over. I wished many times out there in the hot fields that I had been a better scholar.

The hardest work was picking peas. Daddy raised the kind that grew only about six inches off the ground and after bending over all day picking peas, I was ready for bed.

CHAPTER FOUR

Mary

Not long after I went to work in the fields, I met my future wife. Her name was Mary Agnes Varnadore. She lived in Lakeland and worked in the canning plant where my mother worked.

I went to work in the plant after the farming season ended. I was fifteen and Mary sixteen when we met, and by the time I was sixteen I was so madly in love I could barely control myself.

Work in the canning factory wasn't much easier than farming, but there were occasions when it was more fun.

Grapefruit was the big item in our canning factory. Men peeled the fruit and women cut it into sections and packed it in the cans which then went to the cooking room. That's where Mary worked, in the cooking room. My mother was an inspector, and I worked in the shipping department.

The packers worked at a long table which was really a production line. They packed from both sides of the table and were paid not an hourly wage but for how many cans they packed.

When they went to work in the morning, there were plenty of cans, but later in the day cans sometimes became in short supply.

There was a woman on the production line who had a new set of false teeth and one day they were giving her a fit. Her gums were sore and bothered her. They had a large run of grapefruit that day and the woman figured she could make some extra money if she felt more like working, so she slipped the dentures out of her mouth and put them in a can on a shelf behind the line of workers.

Everybody pitched in then, packing grapefruit with a passion, and soon this lady and everyone else had forgotten her teeth.

Later in the day the cans began to run out and in scouting around for more cans, someone grabbed the can off the shelf that held the teeth, packed it with grapefruit, and sent it down the line.

We were loading cases of grapefruit in railroad cars out back when the ladies knocked off for the day and this gal discovered her false teeth were gone.

"Somebody got my teeth," she wailed, and another woman gasped: "I packed that can and sent it to the cooking room."

I don't recall how many hundred cases we had to unload and open up before somebody found the woman's teeth. They had to open the cans, of course, and throw away all that grapefruit.

But it had to be done. Can you imagine what it would do to a grapefruit company if someone opened a can at breakfast and poured out a pound of grapefruit and a set of false teeth?

*   *   *

All this time, Mary and I dated every night, regardless of how late I worked. It didn't matter whether I worked till 6 o'clock or 11 o'clock, I rushed home, ate supper, and drove over to Mary's. We courted until the wee hours of the morning and I got to bed maybe at 3 a.m. Mama woke me at 6 o'clock to get ready to go back to work.

I was young and in love, and the hours didn't matter.

When farming season came again—this was in the summer of 1941—I left the canning factory and went back to the fields.

Mary and I were still seeing each other every night, and finally we got up enough nerve to agree to marry. I was scared to death to approach my dad on this.

There were two strong reasons I wanted to get married: I loved Mary, and I wanted to get off that farm. I wasn't cut out to be a farmer.

It was on a Sunday afternoon that I finally got enough

courage to approach my father. We had finished dinner and he was rocking and smoking on the front porch.

I took a chair beside him and casually said, "Daddy, I think me and Mary are going to get married in five weeks."

He didn't miss a rock. Looking straight at me, he said, "If you're going to get married, why are you going to wait five weeks? Get married now."

Well, I was some relieved, and we quickly switched our plans and prepared to get married the following week.

* * *

We were married June 14, 1941, at camp meeting in Wimauma, Florida, by the Reverend W. C. Bird who later became the father-in-law of my nephew, Donnie Sumner. Donnie went on to sing lead in the Stamps Quartet. I gave him five dollars to marry us. I was sixteen and Mary, seventeen.

Getting married wasn't all that easy, however. Our ages were a problem. When we applied for a marriage license at the Polk County courthouse in Bartow, they would not consider issuing the license because of our ages. The judge told us to go home and work two or three years, save up some money and buy some furniture, then come back and he would marry us.

We didn't even consider taking his advice, but began casting around for another way. If nothing else developed, we would go to Georgia where there was no age limit.

Before going to Georgia, though, we decided to try once more in Florida. Taking my sister, Myrtis, and Mary's mother, we drove to Zephyrhills in Pasco County and at the courthouse there I lied about our ages. I told them I was twenty-one and Mary was twenty. My sister and Mary's mother, knowing we were going to get married anyway, backed my story and saved us a long trip to Georgia. They issued the license.

After the wedding we drove back to Lakeland to set up housekeeping. We bought a case of pork and beans, two loaves of bread, one roll of toilet paper, and some eggs and grits. I had exactly fifty cents left in my pocket.

We rented an apartment from my grandmother for two dollars a week. It had a kitchen and bedroom, and we had privilege of using the bath.

I took a job driving a dump truck for Mary's brother-in-law,

Lewis Roberts, who owned a fleet of twelve trucks. He paid me twelve dollars a week.

The first thing we wanted to do was save a little money, so we hatched up the idea of giving my grandmother two dollars a week and letting her keep it for us. My grandmother was a very frugal person and we knew the money would be safe with her.

For fourteen weeks we saved, and suddenly we needed the twenty-eight dollars for some new furniture. We asked my grandmother for the money and she refused to give it up. She said she would keep it for advance rent.

I had to have my own mother intercede, but we finally got the money.

We had no air conditioning, of course, and it gets awfully hot in Florida in the summertime. Where we lived, the houses were built close together and little air could circulate between them.

In order to sleep, I would take the screen off our bedroom window, put my pillow in the window and sleep with my head on the outside of the house. Brother, it was hot that summer, and the fact that we were amorous young newlyweds didn't cool things off a bit.

We had no idea when or how we would ever get any transportation. We had to ride the bus or walk or borrow the car from my mother and father when we went anywhere.

After about two years, we were able to buy a car. Our first one was a 1935 Plymouth coupe, a dandy little car. I was only eighteen when we bought it, and owning that car gave me a false sense of affluence. Soon after that—this was in 1943—I got a job helping build army bases, first in Dothan, Alabama, then Panama City, Florida, and from there I went to Melbourne, Florida, where I helped build Melbourne Air Force Base. I thought I was pretty prosperous. We lived in a tourist court for a small fee and were living pretty well for the time and place. I went to Lakeland one weekend and, on the spur of the moment, traded our 1935 Plymouth for a pink 1938 Chevrolet. I drove it back to Melbourne—and soon discovered just how prosperous we really were. The first month I couldn't make my payment, and to keep me from losing the car completely, my daddy persuaded the people in Lakeland to take the Chevrolet back and let me have my

Plymouth. I kept the Plymouth until I went in the army in 1944.

Before that, though, Mary and I started acquiring our family. I say acquiring because we adopted our daughter Frances when she was three years old. Frances and Donnie Sumner, who sang with me in the Stamps Quartet, are sister and brother. Their father, Frank Sumner, a cousin of mine, was killed in a beer tavern brawl in the summer of 1943. Seven weeks later, their mother abandoned her four children and left town with a soldier. Donnie was ten months old, Frances was three, their brother Pete was eleven, and there was a thirteen-year-old half-sister, the daughter of their mother by a previous marriage. Frank Sumner's brother, Jimmy, found the children about a week after their mother abandoned them. My brother Buddy, who had no children, adopted Donnie. Mary and I adopted Frances. Pete was taken by his grandfather, and the half-sister was adopted by someone else.

When we got Frances, she had no shoes, one dress, one set of underwear, and was very, very dirty. She had such scales on her head, from a total lack of soap and water, that it took us months to get them out.

When we took her, I wasn't making any money. It was in the summertime and the fruit game was out and I went to a friend named Humphrey Bennett and borrowed twenty-five dollars. The next day Mary and I took Frances to town and spent the money buying clothes for her.

Frances wouldn't talk when we first got her. "I'm your daddy and Mary's your mama," I would tell her. "Do you understand that?" She would nod her head. For a long while she wouldn't talk, she was so scared and, we liked to think, so excited and overwhelmed over her new home and the love we lavished upon her. One day we were giving her a bath and took her out of the tub and stood her up to dry her, and she started singing a hillbilly song, *Pistol-Packin' Mama*, that was popular in that day. "Lay your pistol down, babe, lay your pistol down," she sang, and laughed excitedly. "Pistol-packin' mama, lay your pistol down." This broke the ice, and from that day to this, we've never had another communication problem.

Mary and I had been trying to have a child, and when we took Frances in the summer of 1943, the doctor said Mary got pregnant because of the mother instinct created by the acquisition of Frances. At any rate, our daughter Shirley was born April 26, 1944, and we suddenly had a fine family of two daughters.

There was a lot of difference in the two girls. Frances was quiet and reserved. I don't remember having to whip her but once. That was when she trimmed her eyelashes with a pair of scissors. Shirley was a different story. She had a lot of J. D. in her. She wasn't mean; she was mischievous like most kids.

I don't remember Frances ever asking for but one thing, a little rocking chair. We would take her to the ice cream shop and ask, "Baby, what do you want?" and she'd say, "I don't want anything." "Don't you want a cone of ice cream?" I would ask, and she'd say, "No, sir."

We were downtown one Saturday night in Lakeland and Frances saw a little rocking chair in the window of a furniture store. She pointed to the chair and said she wanted it. It cost fourteen dollars and we were so happy she'd found something she wanted that we bought the chair and didn't have enough money left to eat the next week. I still have the rocking chair and wouldn't take a million dollars for it.

There was a similar incident involving Shirley that had a completely different ending. It was in 1946, after I'd been in the army but before I started singing, we were living in a housing project, and I was unemployed and drawing twenty-one dollars a week compensation. This was in the summer when the fruit business was down.

Shirley was just walking well and went out front to play with some children who had a tricycle. They wouldn't let her ride it and I stood there and watched until I got pretty dog-gone mad.

Shirley was crying and the frustrations of not being able to find a job were building inside me, so I got in my car and went downtown and took my paycheck that I had just received and spent seventeen dollars on a tricycle.

It was such a large tricycle and Shirley was such a little girl that she couldn't ride it. Her feet wouldn't reach the pedals. But she stayed outside on that tricycle and wouldn't get off it till dark. I went out and told her to come in and she wouldn't. I begged her to come in, and she wouldn't, and I started whipping her, and still she wouldn't get off.

I beat her unmercifully, taking out all my frustrations on her. Mary was crying, Frances was crying, Shirley was crying, and I was crying. To this day I regret it, but I'm sure that Shirley understands.

CHAPTER FIVE

Private Sumner

Pearl Harbor was bombed on December 7 following our marriage in June of 1941, and the nation was cast into World War II. I was too young for the draft, so I turned to defense work, helping build those army bases in Alabama and Florida.

When I became old enough to be drafted, I was turned down because of my flat feet. Classified 4F, I took a welding course at night school and got a job welding in the shipyard in Tampa, thirty-two miles from Lakeland where we lived. With the war on, you couldn't change jobs without permission from your draft board, but you could usually get permission if your new job was a hundred percent for the war effort.

I got a new job in Lakeland welding in a factory in which amphibious tanks were built. The new job would save me sixty-four miles of driving every day and all that time I was spending on the road. Too, the new job was strictly for the war effort.

Without going to the draft board for approval, I quit my job in Tampa and went to work in Lakeland. Then I went over to the draft board to tell them.

You'd have thought I hit that draft board in the face with a wet towel. Instead of being pleased that I was going to save the government all that gasoline, the draft board got huffy, changed my classification to 1A, had me reexamined, and evermore put me in the army.

Well, I wasn't too alarmed about that. I was no draft

dodger, and I had wanted to get in service. Today I wouldn't take any amount of money for my experience in the army.

I was inducted February 28, 1944, and took basic training at Camp Sibert near Gadsden and Attalla, Alabama. My feet gave me a fit. They were flat, all right, but I toughed it out. I took a twenty-mile hike in basic and walked the entire distance. I was determined not to fall out like some of the boys did. When I got back to the barracks I couldn't pull my shoes off.

I had to soak shoes, feet, and all in hot water for a long while before the shoes came off. I was never allowed to hike anymore.

My feet still bother me. I remember playing a round of golf in the late 1960s at Beaver Lake Golf Course in Asheville and walked seventeen holes. Eldridge Fox of the Kingsmen Quartet was waiting at the seventeenth and I just got in the car and quit. I couldn't play the last hole, my feet hurt so bad. Usually I ride a golf cart, but they were all in use that day.

Because of my feet, my soldiering became a succession of light duty assignments in army hospitals.

Shirley was born in Lakeland while I was in basic training at Camp Sibert. She was a seven months baby and the news wasn't good when she was born. My sister, Bernice, called me at 4 o'clock in the morning to tell me I was a daddy.

"Mary had a baby," Bernice said, "but I don't want to build up your hopes. The baby just weighs three pounds and eight ounces and the doctor said he doesn't see how it can live, but Mary's all right."

I was glad that Mary was okay, and I sure prayed hard for our baby to live.

When we finished basic training, I was the only one in our outfit who didn't go overseas. We were all waiting in the barracks to be shipped out, wondering where we were going, whether overseas or to another camp for more training or what, when this sergeant came in and walked straight up to me and said, "You lucky so-and-so."

"What is it?" I asked.

"I'm not supposed to tell," he said, "but I'd give my right arm to be going where you're going."

He wouldn't say anymore, but took me to the railroad station, gave me my sealed orders, and put me on the train. Only after the train began to move was I allowed to open my orders. I ripped the envelope open, read the orders quickly, and began to laugh with joy. I was to report to the Breakers Hotel in West Palm Beach, which had been turned into a general hospital. The Breakers Hotel was a classy four-star hotel and rooms in it, at that time, fifty years ago, cost up toward a hundred dollars a night. What duty that was going to be, I thought, and I really looked forward to it. I had a few days before I was to report so I got off the train in Lakeland and headed for the house. I had never seen my baby.

Shirley had stayed in the incubator six weeks and they'd just gotten her out and brought her home when I arrived. Mary was living with my mother and daddy and was absolutely thrilled over our new baby. When she saw me the first thing she did was run and bring the baby for me to see. I've never seen an uglier baby in my life!

"My gosh," I said, "it looks like a rat!"

Mary burst into tears and I had to apologize and tell her I didn't really think the baby looked like a rat, even though I did.

I stayed home a few days, then reported to West Palm Beach. The army assigned me to the motor pool and put me to driving a truck for the hospital. My only duties were to drive that truck to the kitchen of the hotel, back it up to a loading area at 8 a.m., and at 4 p.m. drive the truck to the city dump and empty it.

In a few days I was able to return to Lakeland and bring Mary and the kids to West Palm Beach to live with me.

Shirley wasn't growing. We had her on a strict schedule of so many ounces of milk a day and were following the schedule religiously. Late one afternoon we wrapped Shirley in a blanket and walked down the street toward the movie theater. Shirley was screaming at the top of her voice. A little old lady who must have been eighty stopped us and snapped, "What's wrong with that baby?"

I told her we didn't know, that she was just crying.

"How much does she cry?" the lady asked.

"Most all the time," I said.

"Let me have her a minute." The lady was so abrupt that

Mary handed Shirley over. The woman examined Shirley and looked up with daggers coming out of her eyes. "This baby's starving to death," she said. "How much do you feed her?"

Mary told her and she said, "My goodness! Take this baby back home and feed her something. And from now on, every time this baby cries you check and see if there's a pin sticking in her or if something's choking her, and if it isn't, you give her that bottle."

We did. We went straight back home and fed Shirley. And from then on when she cried Mary gave her the bottle and she quit crying and began gaining weight. She became a real healthy baby.

After several months I was transferred to a general hospital in Charleston, South Carolina, and after I had been there a while I brought Mary and Frances and Shirley up to live with me there. We rented a room for ten dollars a week. No bath, just one room, but we made out all right.

Possibly the most embarrassing moment of my life happened when I reported for duty at Charleston. Each of the barracks buildings there contained sixty beds. It was winter and I wore my Official Dress (OD) uniform. On the left breast of my jacket I pinned the "Expert Rifleman" badge that I had won in basic training for being the third best rifle shot in the 1,200 recruits who had taken that basic training course.

I walked into my barracks when I reported to Charleston wearing my ODs with that rifleman badge on my chest, carrying my duffle bag slung over a shoulder. I was proud of that badge and kept it shined.

There were about fifteen or twenty men sitting around a stove in the middle of the room, talking and smoking, and I went around looking for an empty bunk. When I came up to these men I nodded to them and suddenly one of them got up and came to me, stooped over and peered at the badge on my chest.

So the rest could hear him, he said, "Great Godalmighty, boys, look here: This guy is an expert rifleman and a sharpshooter!"

"Wow!" I heard some of them say. Several got up and came closer to look at the badge.

These were grizzled veterans of Gen. George Patton's Third

army, which had engaged in the Battle of the Bulge and some of the toughest fighting of the war. They were the roughest, toughest soldiers in the world.

The one who had approached me first began to shine my expert rifleman badge with his shirt sleeve, and the others were making comments. I heard one say, "I ain't believin' it. A sharpshooter right here in the barracks! Why, if we'd had him in Europe I'll betcha we'd'a won the war a whole lot sooner."

I was beginning to feel awfully small and when I looked over at the wall and saw all of their uniforms hanging there, I'd never seen so many ribbons and decorations in my life: Purple Hearts, Silver Stars, battle stars, campaign ribbons—every award and decoration you could imagine. There were some Medals of Honor there, too.

I was standing in the middle of a bunch of honest to goodness war heroes!

And at that moment, I could have cried. I remember wishing I could be anywhere but where I was.

All I could think to say—and I guess it was the right thing—was, "Fellows, if you will allow me to take this thing off, I promise you I'll never wear it again!"

Well, they backed off, and I ripped that badge off my chest. I still have it, but I have never pinned it on another jacket of any kind.

A man knows when he's surrounded and needs to surrender. Those were perhaps the greatest fighting men the world had ever known. And to think that I walked into that barracks thinking I was as good as Patton himself—and I'd never shot as much as a sling-shot in combat!

You know, those fellows and I got along after that. I had brought my guitar along, and I used to sit around that stove at night picking and singing gospel songs to those boys, and they were as quiet as mice. If I've ever been engaged in anything that could be called a ministry, I guess that was it, picking and singing to combat veterans who'd been through hell, who were lonely and away from home, most of them shot up and some still suffering from their wounds.

We found a common ground in gospel music and we became buddies before long.

I served there until July 3, 1945, when I was discharged.

I went straight back to Lakeland and started driving an infernal truck again.

CHAPTER SIX

Music in the Early Days

Maybe it has sounded so far as if there were little or no music in my life. My mother and father had no special musical inclination, and it didn't noticeably run in the family, but all this time my voice was getting deeper and deeper.

I had been singing with quartets as long as I could remember, just messing around. We sang at churches and camp meetings, and it was with a church quartet when I was eleven that I sang on the first radio program ever broadcast over Radio Station WLAK in Lakeland.

I was in the fifth grade. We formed a quartet made up of my sister, Myrtis; my double first cousin, Marjorie Sumner (my dad and his brother had married sisters); another cousin, Opal Hicks, and myself. I sang bass.

We were each given a box of candy for singing on that WLAK program. That was the first pay I ever got for singing.

*   *   *

Before I went to the army, something happened that would help me get into singing after the war.

Stacy Selph, a singer of some note, was going to the army, too, and before he left, a group in Lakeland gave a singing in his honor in the Lakeland High School auditorium one Sunday afternoon. I attended, of course, and being a bass singer, I was invited to be on the program. This is where Stacy first noticed me, and it led to his recommending me later for my first professional singing job.

Before that, I had been given a big thrill at a singing in that same auditorium one Sunday afternoon. Through the

48

week we used to move around from church to church, but on Sundays the singing conventions were held in high schools in the area.

Television had not yet been perfected and not every family had a radio, so the singing conventions were a large part of our entertainment. When the weeknight sing came to my church, I could show off my voice a little more than I would in the other fellow's church, and folks began to notice.

Vivian Selph, president of the Polk County Singing Convention, was on stage that Sunday afternoon when I walked into the Lakeland High School auditorium. He stopped what he was saying, and said, "Folks, a great bass singer has just come in." Everybody looked around, and Vivian added, "Come on down front, J. D., and get in the choir."

I don't think I ever felt any taller than I did walking down the aisle with everybody looking at me and Vivian waiting until I got in the choir to go on with the program.

*   *   *

There wasn't any singing in my life while I was in the army, except that little bit I did for the Third Army at Charleston, but it didn't take me long to get back in the groove once the army let me go. My first big break in singing came through Stacy Selph in 1945. The Sunny South Quartet, which could probably be called the forerunner of the Rebels Quartet, was operating out of Tampa. Big Chief James Wetherington, later bass singer for the Statesmen for twenty-five years, was singing bass for the Sunny South. Horace Floyd was the tenor; Mosie Lister, the songwriter, was the baritone; Lee Kitchens the lead; and Quintin Hicks the piano player.

As a lot of quartets did in those days, these fellows had a bust-up. Big Chief, Mosie, and Lee Kitchens pulled out and started a quartet known as the Melody Masters.

Horace was manager of the Sunny South. He immediately hired Stacy Selph for the lead and Joe Thomas for baritone. Stacy recommended me and Horace gave me my first job as a bass singer with a professional quartet.

We sang that way for a while and were starving to death. The Melody Masters remained in the area and they, too, had eating problems.

Times were hard. We hadn't quite reached the post-war

boom. In fact, it took people in gospel singing a while longer to get into the good times than those in other fields.

I wasn't making a living singing, but I didn't want to quit, so I enrolled in a school to learn watchmaking and supplemented my singing pay through the G. I. Bill of Rights. I took the entire course, and continued to sing at night. That way, Mary and I managed to make ends meet—barely.

Stacy finally had to quit, and when he did we hired an Alabama boy named Jake Hess to sing the lead. Jake, who was developing into a great singer, had been with the John Daniels Quartet, one of the leading groups of that day.

We hired a new baritone named Roger Clark. He was a Texan, had attended the Stamps School of Music, and was singing with the Stamps Quartet, with singers the caliber of Harley Lester, Loy Hooker, and Glen Payne.

The first night Jake was with us, we had an engagement at a church in Auburndale, Florida, and sixteen people showed up. Jake and I walked out to the front of the church just before the program began and he said to me, "George," he nicknamed me George, "which way is Haleyville from here?" Haleyville, Alabama, was his home and he acted as if he were about to take off because he thought he had hooked on with a loser.

Loser or not, there was one department that Jake and I intended to win in. We grew mustaches. I thought if I was going to be a bass singer of any note, I had to grow a mustache. Everybody else did. So Jake and I let our mustaches grow and we'd hack and trim them to shape them the way we wanted.

We had an office in the back of a printing shop and when our mustaches didn't grow as fast as we wanted them to, we'd sneak into the printing shop and paint them with printer's ink.

Jake's didn't last, but I've worn a mustache to this day. It's a part of me.

Jake didn't stay with us very long. He went with the Melody Masters, and they had their hard luck story, too. At that time the Melody Masters consisted of Calvin Newton, tenor; Jake, lead; Alvin Toodle, baritone; Big Chief, bass; and Wally Varner on the piano.

Eventually they moved to Greenville, South Carolina, in an

effort to improve their lot. Jake told me later that in Greenville things were so tough they once went three days without eating and wound up stealing peaches to keep from starving to death.

Hovie Lister always called Big Chief "a great quartet man" and the reason is that Big Chief was one of the survivors of that day when you had to be a dedicated quartet man just to exist in our business.

There were other changes in personnel coming up, and in quartets for me.

The Sunny South Quartet was sponsored by the Dixie Lily Company, largest milling company in Florida. We sang over Radio Station WFLA in Tampa and went on the road in a DeSoto Suburban, a big three-seated car that would haul seven people rather comfortably. Cecil Webb, president of Dixie Lily, bought the car for us.

Station WORZ in Orlando, a 5,000-watt station, made us an offer to move there and despite the fact that Horace Floyd, our manager, didn't like it, we agreed the offer was too good to turn down. So we moved.

But Horace just couldn't take it. He backed out of the deal and decided to return to WFLA in Tampa where he could sing and work as a salesman for the station. So we all returned to Tampa.

Not long after that, Horace decided to switch to Orlando again, this time to WOOF, a larger station than WORZ, and when he went he took the name of the Sunny South Quartet with him. He was the manager, remember.

I stayed in Tampa and organized the Dixie Lily Harmoneers. I hired Horace Parrish and John Matthews, both of whom put in twenty years with the Rebels after that. I got Joe Thomas to join us and picked up a boy named Ray Mercer to play the piano.

John Matthews is my brother-in-law, married to my sister Myrtis.

There wasn't a great deal of money in singing in those days and some of us stayed in it at the expense of better jobs and the welfare of our families. I was guilty of that. My family was starving.

My mother, who always canned a lot of food, had put up some old red beans that my daddy absolutely refused to eat—

and if he wouldn't eat them, they were pretty low on the totem pole.

We were living in a housing project on 22nd Avenue in Tampa, and I went off to sing many a night and left my family with nothing to eat but those old beans and water without ice.

I think that's the only time Mary really became disgusted with my singing. I'm sure it was discouraging for her, me wanting to sing so badly and not wanting to work like other men.

One evening she reached the boiling point. She and Frances and Shirley were sitting in the kitchen eating those beans and drinking that warm water, and as I was about to leave, Mary had about as much as she could take.

"If you don't think any more of me and the kids than to let us live like this when you could be out working," she said, "if you go sing tonight, when you get back home I won't be here."

I looked around the living room. My coat was lying on an old couch that my mother had given us. We'd lost our furniture with me trying to sing for a living. But I was determined to sing. There never was a man with more determination.

"You can learn a lesson of a lifetime if you just watch me," I said to Mary. "Just as long as my legs point toward the ground, I'm going to sing."

I put on my coat and left.

When I returned home later that night after singing, Mary was still there. She was sitting at the bottom of the stairs crying and I walked in and put my arm around her and said, "Now, Mary, I'm going to sing as long as I live. I want you to know that I love you very much, but don't ever ask me not to sing again."

Until the day she died, she never mentioned me not singing again. I'm sure she wasn't afraid to, but things became better. She was just pushed up against the wall that night, and I'm proud to say Mary was such a woman that she stuck through thick and thin with my singing without further complaint.

I managed the Dixie Lily Harmoneers until 1949 when I went with the Sunshine Boys.

I've Got That Old Time Religion in My Heart and *If We Never Meet Again* were big songs for us. So were *I'll Meet You in the Morning, Did You Ever Go Sailing? Little*

Pine Log Cabin, Glad Reunion Day, and *Marching Up to Heaven.*

Those were great days, though tough ones. As late as 1949, after I had been singing professionally four years, I had only two shirts and one suit.

The suit was sharkskin and the seat of the pants was ripped. Each day before I went to the studio, I put a strip of tape over the rip to hide my backside.

We had two radio programs a day, one at 7 in the morning and the other at noon. At night we usually sang in concert somewhere and while I was gone Mary would wash my other shirt so I would have a clean one to wear the next day.

*   *   *

My first recording session was with the Sunny South Quartet. We did *Glad Reunion Day* and *Marching Up to Heaven* on the White Church label. Before that we had no records, we traveled in a beat-up 1937 Plymouth, and tried to supplement our singing income by selling song books for the Stamps Quartet Music Company.

White Church was the first recording company to do anything major in the field of gospel music. It recorded the Homeland Harmony Quartet—Lee Roy Abernathy, Connor Hall, Shorty Bradford, Aycel Soward, and James McCoy—on such songs as *The Gospel Boogie* and *Burning of the Winecoff Hotel,* which Lee Roy wrote, and *Lord, I'm Feeling Mighty Fine* and *Checking Up on My Payments to the Lord,* which the Sunshine Boys also recorded after I joined them.

White Church's number one group at the time, I suppose, was the Rangers Quartet, which was also considered to be tops in the business.

Soon after cutting our record for White Church, we went up to Jacksonville one Sunday to work a singing convention with the Rangers.

Their personnel included Arnold Hyles, the great bass singer known as the lowest in the world; Denver Crumpler, billed as the highest tenor; Arnold's brother, Vernon Hyles, an excellent lead singer who could get on down as low as most basses; Walter Leverett on the baritone; and Doy Ott at the piano.

They were a tremendous quartet.

I was just a kid, maybe twenty-two years old, and I idolized
Arnold Hyles. I thought just to be around him was the greatest
thing in the world.

During the noon hour when no one was singing on the
stage, they played records over the loudspeaker, and most of
what they played were of the Rangers and Homeland Harmony.

After a while, they put the Sunny South's recording on and
played *Marching Up to Heaven,* which had a bass lead. As
usual, I was following Arnold around, walking right behind
him, and when I hit that bass lead on the recording, he
stopped in his tracks and I almost ran over him.

He turned around very slowly and asked, "Boy, is that you?"

Well, I was so dumbfounded that he would notice that I
couldn't answer him. I tried to swallow and couldn't. I never
did answer him; I just nodded my head. He turned back
around and went on his way, but right then I knew that I had
answered my calling. His noticing my singing was a tremendous encouragement to me.

*   *   *

There in the late 1940s quartets had no qualms about battling each other for prominence. Prominence meant survival,
and survival was worth fighting for. At least, that's the way
we all figured it.

When the Melody Masters split off from the Sunny South
in 1946, they went to St. Petersburg to sing over WSUN. We
in the Sunny South—Horace Floyd, Jake Hess, Joe Thomas,
Quintin Hicks, and I—were on WFLA in Tampa. Not only
were we competing quartets, our stations were competing
stations.

Our two quartets fought one another tooth and nail for
popularity in the bay area. On stage, we didn't like each
other at all, in a childish way, I guess. It was professional
jealousy on both our parts. There was no fist-swinging animosity between us. At least, we never came to blows. We got
along right well off stage.

I borrowed my daddy's 1942 Chevrolet one Sunday to drive
our quartet to the Arcadia Singing Convention. Big Chief and
the Melody Masters had a 1946 Nash. They had no place to

sing that day and knew that we did, but they didn't know exactly where we were going.

They knew which direction we were going, though, because when we left Tampa they were waiting for us on the side of the road. I was driving and when we passed, they took off behind us. Soon we figured out that they were going to follow us to the convention but didn't know where it was.

I tried to outrun them. I pushed that Chevy up to eighty-five, ninety miles an hour, and Big Chief stayed right with us. He would have made a good race car driver; he always had a heavy foot.

Joe Thomas lived in a place called Wauchula, between Tampa and Arcadia, so we stopped at his house to outwait them. They pulled on down the road and stopped.

They didn't know there was a back road out of Joe's place that we could take without letting them see us, so we left by that way and drove on to Arcadia, fifteen or twenty miles away.

We arrived at 11 o'clock, in plenty of time for dinner-on-the-ground, and the Melody Masters didn't find the place till 4 in the afternoon. We were finished by then.

*   *   *

We did a hatchet job on the Melody Masters at a singing convention in Okeechobee, Florida, one Sunday, employing one of the favorite tricks of the time.

Both the Melody Masters and the Sunny South had been invited to sing at this convention and we purposely arrived a little late so the Melody Masters would have to sing first.

They were on stage and going rather well when we got there, and we waited outside until just the right moment. There was a speaker from the P. A. set on the inside of the church and a speaker on the outside to take care of the over-flow if the church filled up.

At the opportune moment, we picked up our song books and walked in the front door of the church and right down the aisle.

As we entered, our fans saw us and began clapping their hands. We shook hands and spoke to people all the way down the aisle and completely tore up the Melody Masters' stand.

In times like that, when our Christian consciences began

to balk, we usually soothed them with the thought that the Melody Masters would gladly have performed the same hatchet job on us had we arrived first.

This business of battling for prominence reached all the way to the top in gospel music of that day.

Frank Stamps, whose Stamps Quartet Music Company was represented by the Sunny South Quartet as song book salesmen, used to visit his quartets once in a while. One year he chose the Florida State Singing Convention for his visit to the Sunny South Quartet.

The Melody Masters represented the rival Stamps-Baxter Music Company.

Both of our quartets were pretty hot then.

At this convention, like other conventions of that day, the stage was filled with chairs and all the singers sat on stage facing the audience. When a quartet was called to sing, its members simply rose and stepped to the microphone.

The Melody Masters were called first that day—and they really turned it on. They had that crowd rocking in no time at all.

No one on stage doubted that the Melody Masters would be a hard act to follow that afternoon.

Well, almost no one.

Frank Stamps had other ideas.

As soon as he saw how the Melody Masters were going, he got out of his chair and headed across the stage toward the water fountain. His path took him directly over the wire that connected the P. A. set to the nearest electrical outlet.

Just as he stepped across the wire, he hooked a toe in it and jerked—and unplugged the P. A.

The Melody Masters suddenly went dead. They found themselves singing to a dead mike. No one could hear them. They turned around to see what was wrong and Mr. Stamps shrugged his shoulders and spread his hands.

"Gee, fellows," he said, "I sure am sorry."

By the time someone plugged up the P. A. set again, the crowd had lost most of its edge and the Melody Masters couldn't recover during that stand.

And Mr. Stamps was standing off stage chuckling.

The Sunny South had a deal with the Stamps Quartet Music Company that gave us sixty percent of the revenue from our song book sales, and the other forty percent went to the company.

Mr. Stamps decided once that he'd change that policy, switching it directly around. He notified us that henceforth we could keep forty percent and send sixty to him.

We balked, of course. Being hot-headed, I got mad. I was in charge of our song book sales and had thousands of books in the storeroom.

I boxed up all of them and took them over to the Tampa Airport and sent them back to him C.O.D. by air express. It must have cost three thousand dollars to ship them back.

The odd part of this story was that later on the Stamps Quartet Music Company almost went bankrupt and James and Cecil Blackwood and I bought it from Mr. Stamps. I have often wondered whether we had to absorb that air express bill. We probably did.

CHAPTER SEVEN

The Sunshine Boys

My next upward step came early in 1949 when Ace Richman of the Sunshine Boys called Horace Floyd in Orlando and told him that he needed a bass singer and a first tenor. Horace told Ace that he was interested in the tenor job and that he knew of a good bass he would bring along.

Horace drove to Tampa and asked me if I wanted to go to Atlanta and join the Sunshine Boys. The Dixie Lily Harmoneers still weren't making any money to speak of, so I told Horace I would go.

To the disappointment of my wife and my mother and father, I left the Harmoneers, rented a trailer, hooked it to the back of my 1941 Chevrolet and loaded what junky furniture we had into the trailer. We headed for Atlanta.

On the way we ran into one of those South Georgia gully-washers. It stormed so quick and so hard that I couldn't get to a filling station fast enough and part of our furniture was ruined.

We made it to Atlanta and Ace rented us a house for twenty-five dollars a month. It was no bargain. I'll never forget how dirty that house was. I tried to paint it but it was so dirty that by the time I got the brush over it and looked back the black would be leaking through the paint. I wound up literally throwing paint on the walls, but we made the house livable.

The Smith brothers, Tennessee and Smitty, had just quit the Sunshine Boys, who were singing over Radio Station WSB. Ace and Eddie Wallace and the Smiths owned the name "Sunshine Boys," and when they broke up they were so mad at each other that the Smiths wouldn't let us use the name.

So we called ourselves the Travelers Quartet until things blew over and the rift between Ace and the Smiths narrowed. Finally, when the Smiths didn't care any longer we resumed the name of the Sunshine Boys.

Horace sang tenor, Eddie was the lead, Ace the baritone, and I the bass. There were only four of us; Eddie played piano.

Horace didn't stay long. He didn't like Atlanta, so he went back to Orlando and we heard that Freddie Daniels of Covington, Georgia, was a good tenor. We contacted him and he turned out to be just that, and a good fellow, too, so Ace hired him.

We stayed in Atlanta almost a year, performing on the WSB Barn Dance with James and Martha Carson, but when that show folded we discovered we were paddling that same old canoe: we were starving again.

We decided to become the Sunshine Boys again and to look for greener pastures, so Ace, Eddie, Freddie, and I got in the car, left our wives in Atlanta—we were flat broke, all but Ace—and went out to find a new place to work.

In Charlotte we tried WBT but found no satisfaction. We went to WRVA in Richmond and to KDKA in Pittsburgh and it was the same story.

Finally, we hit Wheeling, West Virginia, and got a job singing on WWVA. This was in December of 1949, just before Christmas, and after some early struggling, which we were used to, the Sunshine Boys turned out to be the most popular group WWVA had known. We stayed in Wheeling till late 1951.

We sang regularly on the WWVA Jamboree, which almost everybody within range listened to. It was something like the Grand Ole Opry, and, in fact, a lot of the entertainers on the Jamboree, like Wilma Lee and Stoney Cooper, Hawkshaw Hawkins, and a bunch of others, migrated from there to the Opry.

Ace, Fred, Eddie, and I moved into one room on Wheeling Island which sits in the Ohio River, the dividing line for the states of Ohio and West Virginia.

I had to borrow money for food. We each lived on a dollar

and fifteen cents a day. We ate only twice a day, spending forty cents for breakfast and seventy-five cents for a hamburger steak later.

Our routine developed quickly. We got up early and walked across the bridge to Wheeling proper where the station was located and sang a 7 a.m. show. Ace had a 1941 Chevrolet coupe which we had driven up to Wheeling, and we had a company car, a worn-out 1948 Buick convertible. But we couldn't afford to buy gas for either, so we walked.

After singing on the 7 o'clock program, we ran back to our room and went back to bed, staying in bed as long as we could. We would stay right there until we got so hungry we couldn't stand it, then we'd get up and go to the restaurant and spend the forty cents for breakfast.

Then we waited as long as we could until night, and ate the hamburger steaks. That way, we got by on two meals a day.

We got up at 6 one morning to make our 7 o'clock program and it was snowing and there was ice on the bridge.

"George, where's your overcoat?" Ace asked me.

I still had the sharkskin suit with the tape on the trousers.

"You can't go without your overcoat," Ace said.

I looked at him. "Don't let it shake you," I said, "but I've never owned an overcoat in my life." We didn't know what overcoats were in Florida.

Ace, Eddie, and Freddie already had their overcoats on and buttoned and were ready to go, but Ace began to shuck his. "Take off your coats," he said. "If George doesn't wear an overcoat, neither do we."

So they removed their topcoats and the three of us walked across that freezing bridge to work.

*   *   *

We figured we had a chance to make some money in Wheeling if we played things right. WWVA was a 50,000-watt station and we knew we were reaching out. But we decided that we would not begin playing concerts until we became known and popular enough to draw good crowds. We gave ourselves a month during which we would make no personal appearances, and see how things worked out. On the air, Ace plugged the fact that the Sunshine Boys would soon begin appearing in concert and invited anyone who wanted to book us to write to the station.

Meanwhile, things were still going poorly. I had not made any money in my singing career. I was eleven hundred dollars in debt when we went to Wheeling.

My mother and dad insisted we come home for Christmas in 1949, even though we had just taken the job in Wheeling. I made my way back to Atlanta where I had a beat-up 1941 Chevrolet two-seater. So Mary and I and our two babies, Frances and Shirley, got in the car and headed for Florida.

In Monticello, Florida, the Chevrolet's engine gave way. A rod came out of it and I spent twenty-one dollars to have a new one put in. The new rod lasted fifty miles, and it came out in Perry, Florida.

At that moment, I had two dollars and sixty cents in my pocket and that was all that stood between us and the wolf at the door.

I found a telephone and called my mother's house. Nell Sumner, Buddy's wife and John Matthews' sister (that's another case where brother and sister married sister and brother), answered the phone and I told her to send Buddy up to Perry after us.

Buddy and John drove up and pushed my car on to Lakeland.

When we got to Lakeland and had eaten, I had twenty cents left, I was twelve hundred miles from Wheeling, I had no money to get back to my job, my car was torn up, and I had no Christmas presents for my babies.

That was the lowest moment of my life.

But we salvaged what we could. We borrowed enough money for a fairly decent Christmas which we had at my daddy's house.

After Christmas, my daddy borrowed some money from my uncle and I caught a train back to Wheeling. I left Mary and the children in Lakeland, by then twelve hundred dollars in debt.

*   *   *

I got back to Wheeling in early January, 1950, and things immediately began to take a turn for the better. I had never made more than fifteen dollars in any week from singing, and I could hardly believe our sudden good fortune.

We began to accept concert dates and soon found ourselves working three times a day in addition to our radio show. We would sometimes do three churches on Sunday, and through the week we would book a civic club for a luncheon or an early-evening show the same night we had a concert scheduled in the same town.

The clubs would pay us sixty to seventy-five dollars for an appearance, and we were beginning to make good money at our concerts. There were times when so many people showed up for them that we would put on one show, empty the house, fill it up again, and put on a second performance.

The people loved our singing. They listened to us on radio and loved to hear us in person. And we always gave them a good show, with plenty of singing and a lot of comedy. We could entertain a crowd and we didn't always do it with gospel. We sang everything.

We were each making seventy-five to eighty dollars a day, and it was unbelievable.

Each night I would take out the money I needed to live on and mail the rest to Mary in Lakeland.

She was living with my folks and my father couldn't understand my sudden good fortune. He had my mother write me for him.

"Son," she wrote as he dictated, "I don't know what you're doing, but I know what you're doing can't be right. I haven't raised you this way. I raised you to be a good boy and there are other ways you can make your living. If you'll quit whatever you're doing and come back home, I'll support you the rest of my life without you having to do whatever you're doing."

He thought I was stealing!

I had a hard time convincing him that the Sunshine Boys were making a legitimate living. At one time the mail was stopped somewhere between Wheeling and Lakeland and Mary received three envelopes in one mail that contained almost two hundred fifty dollars. For us, that was a big amount of money.

Within a month, Mary paid off the twelve hundred dollars

we owed, had a new engine put in my car, and soon she and the kids came to Wheeling to live with me.

* * *

Our daughter Shirley has special memories of Wheeling. We lived in an old brownstone, and almost all of the Jamboree performers lived in that apartment area. Our apartment was on the top floor and had tall windows across the back. Under the windows were window seats, and Shirley kept her toys piled there. She would play for hours looking out the windows. She had as many cars as dolls, and she played Annie Oakley every day. She was about a first-grader then. She and Gary Daniels, Freddie's son, would chase each other up and down the back stairs of the apartment building until their tongues hung out. Their companions also included Carol Lee Cooper and other show brats.

Mary would sit at her dresser every night brushing her long, beautiful auburn hair a hundred strokes or more. She always told Shirley and Frances that if they wanted beautiful hair they should brush it at least a hundred strokes every night.

Secretly, Shirley always wanted to look like her mother. She thought Mary looked like the movie star, Susan Hayward. Mary was French, and she was always slender and dainty.

Shirley says she can still remember the lingering fragrance of the White Shoulders perfume Mary would wear. Mary also used Coty face powder, and when Shirley grew up, she began using the same thing.

"It is still packaged in the same container I remember on my mother's dresser through the years," Shirley said, "and the smell will always be a part of me. Every day of my life when I use my Coty, the vision, the aroma, and every little thing about my mother's female ritual of sitting at her dresser and 'getting ready' returns to me."

* * *

Shortly after we began playing concerts and before success struck us full force, we bought a 1947 Cadillac limousine that had a worn-out wheel bearing.

We had the car insured and as soon as we realized we'd bought a lemon, we began to hope we could drive it hard enough to catch the bearing on fire and burn up the car. Then we'd collect the insurance and get a better ride.

What we were trying to do was wrong and we knew it, but we were still at the stage of the game where we thought we had to play it this way or go out of business.

We drove the dickens out of that limo, giving her every chance to catch fire on the open road, but she just laughed at us and kept rolling along.

Finally, when we had about given up on the idea of the fire, we were driving through Pennsylvania, low on gasoline, so we pulled into a filling station and just about the time we got out of the car . . . Whoosh! . . . she caught fire.

We grabbed our suitcases and threw them out and shoved the car out in the street so it wouldn't catch the gas tanks on fire. We were pretty happy about it and were going to let her burn.

All of a sudden, a building across the street opened up and I have never seen so many firefighters pile out of one place in my life.

In three minutes there must have been five hundred men putting out that fire with enough chemical equipment to douse a three-alarm fire.

We stood there dumbfounded, looking at each other and then at the car. The old limo had really pulled one over on us. After giving her all those chances to burn on the open road, the place she chose to catch fire was right in front of the Pennsylvania Firefighters School.

A man we took to be their leader came over when the fire was extinguished and with a broad smile of accomplishment on his face, extended his hand. We had to shake hands and thank him while wishing we could wring his neck.

We made the rest of that trip in a very soggy car.

*   *   *

When we finally began making money, the first thing we did was trade off the old cars and buy some good transportation. We bought a 1949 Packard which served us well until a fellow smashed into it in Hagerstown, Pennsylvania. He hit us right between the doors and demolished our car—his, too— but miraculously no one was hurt.

For a while then, we rode a 1942 Cadillac until we bought a 1949 seven-passenger Cadillac.

The limousine had a glass partition separating the rear seats from the driver's seat. The partition could be rolled up and down, but only from the rear seat.

The program director at WWVA at that time was Paul Meyer, who kept wanting to go to one of our concerts with us. The station was in the Holly Building which had a parking garage in the basement where we kept the Cadillac.

We were getting to be cut-ups because we were in the chips and could afford a little fun.

Paul kept bugging us and finally we let him make a trip with us. We all went downstairs together and when the attendant brought out the Cadillac, we four singers jumped in the back seat, locked the doors and rolled up the partition. We made Paul drive us to our concert and wouldn't roll the glass down to talk to him at all. That's how screwy we were.

Pete Cassell, the blind country-western singer, was on WWVA at the same time the Sunshine Boys were and we liked him very much. He had no eyeballs, but he was the most competent blind person I ever knew.

We felt sorry for him and would take him along on some of our concerts, paying him fifteen dollars a night. He couldn't get any dates by himself, of course.

I did most of the driving for the Sunshine Boys, and Pete liked to ride in the front seat with me. The other three guys would sit in the back.

Now and then, we would dig up a race on the highway and Pete, though blind, got a kick out of it. He'd sit there feeling the power of the throbbing engine and say, "Where we at now? Where's he at? Where's he AT?"

"We're even with him," I would say.

"Push it down, push it down," Pete would say. "Push it to the floor!"

He'd get a real bang out of it when we passed a car in a race.

We worked a date in Parkersburg, West Virginia, one night and had to pull into a pretty tight parking place. To show how much humor Pete had, when we finished and were ready to head for home, I started to back out and asked, "How is it back there?"

None of the Sunshine Boys said a word. They sat there like three kings.

"Come on, fellows," I said, "somebody tell me how it is on the right hand side." I could see on the left.

When no one responded, Pete opened his door, stuck his head out, and said, "Come on back. I can't see a thing.

*   *   *

Soon after we bought the seven-passenger Cadillac, we parked it one day in a lot alongside the Holly Building. The station was on the tenth floor and some of us were standing at the window looking at the car down in the lot.

Pete came in and asked what we were doing. We told him we were looking at our new car.

"What kind is it?" he asked. "Where's it at?"

We told him. "It's a black seven-passenger Cadillac, and it's sitting in the second row in the parking lot."

"All right," Pete said. "What's sitting to the left of it?"

"A green Plymouth."

"What's to the right?"

"A red Chevrolet."

"Okay," Pete said. "It's in the second row. How many cars from the end?"

We told him ten cars from the end and went on back in the studio to rehearse.

Pete was standing there like he was looking down at the parking lot when he heard Paul Meyer come in. Pete could identify a person by the sound of his footsteps.

"Hello, Mr. Meyer," he said.

"Hi, Pete," said Paul. "How you doing?"

"I'm looking at the Sunshine Boys' new car," Pete said.

Well, that got Paul's attention. To himself he said, *What do you mean, looking at a car, you cat? You can't see.*

But to Pete he said, "They got a new car, huh?"

"Yeah," Pete said, "and it's a beauty, man. Come here and look at it."

Paul walked over there and looked down toward the parking lot. "Which one is it?"

"It's that Cadillac down there," Pete said, "the black one. See it, second row, see right down here, the black Cadillac, seven-passenger job."

"I don't see it," Paul said.

"Look," said Pete, sounding a bit exasperated. "See the green Plymouth? It's on the left of the Cadillac. See it?"

"Yeah, I see it," Paul said, looking at Pete with a puzzled stare.

"Do you see the red Chevrolet on the right of it?" Pete asked. "In the second row. Look, count ten cars from the end. . . ."

That was enough. Paul came back through the studio shaking his head. "Man, I ain't believing it," he said, "but I thought that cat was blind. He just pointed out your new car and told me what color it was."

CHAPTER EIGHT

Hollywood

The Sunshine Boys prospered. We signed a recording contract with Decca. Our calendar was completely filled with bookings and we were on the road almost every night. Only now and then did we take a night off to rest. Our harmony was tremendous—as good as that of any singing group in the country, including the Sons of the Pioneers.

Then Hollywood beckoned.

We signed a contract with Columbia Pictures to make movies with cowboy stars Charles Starrett and Smiley Burnette. In all, the Sunshine Boys appeared as singing cowboys in seventeen Westerns, but I was not in all of them. I didn't stay with the Sunshine Boys that long.

When we got a call from California, we dropped what we were doing and headed west. Usually Columbia gave us three or four days' notice, which was just about enough time to drive to California.

We bought a new 1950 Packard and had just broken it in when we got a call from Columbia to make a picture with Starrett and Burnette called *Prairie Roundup*. That was in July of 1950. We had a concert date in Atlanta, so we sang there and then took off for Hollywood to make the picture.

We had to be there in three days so we drove straight through in fifty hours from Atlanta to Hollywood—and in 1950, before superhighways, that was moving on!

We went out famous old Route 66, the main east-west artery in the West, stopping only for fuel and food. Usually we bought Vienna sausages, soda crackers, and pop, and hit out again, eating on the go.

68

Eddie Wallace was driving on a stretch through the desert in Arizona and it was blistering hot. We didn't have air conditioning in the car. We were required to wear our hair extremely long; if we didn't, the bright movie lights pierced right through it. A thin place in your hair would appear to be a bald spot on the black and white film.

Ace, sitting up front with Eddie, got warm and cracked his window. The breeze apparently cooled him off a little, so he rolled the window on down.

I was sitting directly behind Ace and the wind coming in his window began flipping my long hair back and forth.

"Roll up the glass, Ace," I said. "It's bugging me."

"You go jump in the lake," Ace said.

The air from his window wasn't bothering anyone but me, so I decided since my hair was flapping around, I might as well roll down my window, too.

When I did, it created a small whirlwind in the car. I looked over at Freddie, who was sitting in back with me, and his hair began to stand up and prance around.

"Come on, boys," Freddie said. "Let's roll the windows up."

Neither Ace nor I would roll up our glasses. We were both mad by this time, and Freddie was getting mad. Eddie was laughing at us. He was still sheltered from the whirlwind.

Freddie asked three or four times for us to roll up the windows and we wouldn't, so he cranked his window down, and with a big puff, the wind stirred up Eddie and Ace's hair.

"Come on, fellows," Eddie yelled. "Roll up the windows!"

We just sneered at him.

So down went his window.

Can you imagine four nuts riding ninety miles an hour across the desert with all the windows down and our manes beating us to death?

Next filling station we pulled into, the attendant started to run. He thought we were escapees from the circus. We told him we were going to Hollywood and he said from the looks of things, Hollywood was certainly the place for us.

*   *   *

We arrived in Hollywood on Sunday morning to be singing cowboys the next day, and Freddie dropped a bombshell. He told us he had never ridden a horse.

To remedy that, we went directly to a riding stable, rented four horses and spent the day trying to teach Freddie how to stay in the saddle. We rode him all day, and he fell into bed that night.

Early Monday morning we drove about forty miles out of Hollywood to the film location.

We were cast as good guys with Charles Starrett and had to take part in a running gunfight. The director put Freddie and me up on one side of the valley so we could ride down the hill, and Ace and Eddie on the other side. We were supposed to charge the rustlers as they came through a pass and make it appear that we were catching up with them.

To ride a horse with a pistol in your hand, you've got to hold the gun in one hand, the reins in the other, and know how to keep your balance and make the horse go where you want him to, mostly with pressure from your knees.

This can be difficult for an experienced rider; it can be maddening if you've never sat a horse until the previous day.

And those horses were nobody's fools; they could tell whether you knew anything about riding. The horse that drew Freddie Daniels that day knew exactly what he had gotten— and he must've wished he was somewhere else.

I had ridden quite a lot and had no problem. We were to go full blast straight to the bottom of the hill, whip around a big oak tree and head down the valley in chase of the rustlers.

The tree was at the foot of the hill and we had to start making our turn just before we got to it. I made it easily, but Freddie didn't know how to gauge his turn, and his horse wasn't telling, so he galloped directly under the tree.

There was a low-hanging limb that the horse had no trouble going under—but Freddie did. The limb struck him just above the eye and knocked him sideways in the saddle.

Here we came, tearing down this valley after the rustlers, and the director did a double take when he saw Freddie come out from under that tree, in full view of the camera's eye, sideways in the saddle, one foot out of a stirrup and canted upward at a sharp angle. He was holding the reins and his hat on his head with his left hand, and shooting up the sky and much of the countryside with the pistol in his right hand.

His balance was precarious, to put it mildly.

I would hesitate to relate what I think was on that director's mind as he came running from behind the camera, waving his arms to stop the cameras and the action.

Freddie's bronc came to a stiff-legged halt near the director and Freddie tumbled to the ground.

"You!" the director stabbed a finger at Freddie. "Have you ever been on a horse before?"

"Oh, yes, sir," Freddie answered.

"When?"

"Well, ah, yesterday, I guess," Freddie mumbled.

The director was seething, and the rest of us weren't laughing—at least, not openly—because movie-making was new to us and we didn't know how seriously to take this man.

"You have never ridden anything but a bicycle," the director shouted at Freddie. "I don't want to catch you near another horse during this picture."

A cowboy took over Freddie's horse and we went on down the canyon and caught up with the rustlers. According to the script, they leaped off their horses and holed up in the rocks, shooting at us.

The director, feeling Freddie couldn't disrupt things any more if he didn't let him near the horses, put Freddie in the gun battle.

Freddie has big, long front teeth, and he has to close his mouth pretty tightly to keep his teeth from showing under normal conditions.

We were facing the sun to take advantage of all the light they could get for close-up shots, and every now and then they put the camera on each of us while we shot at the rustlers.

When Freddie looked into the sun he instinctively squinched his eyes, which drew up the skin from his mouth, and his teeth gleamed brightly.

Freddie and I were behind the same big rock, blazing away with our six-guns. The cameraman zoomed in on Freddie, and suddenly the director yelled, "Cut! . . . Stop! . . . Hold it!"

We stopped shooting.

The director walked over to Freddie. "What are you smiling about?" he asked. "You're in a gun battle. Those other guys are trying to blow your head off." He really sounded exasperated, like he was at the end of his rope.

"I'm not smiling," Freddie said.

"You're not smiling?" the director said. He moved around until the sun was at his back. "Look at me," he said to Freddie.

Freddie looked at him—into the sun—and his eyes squinched, and his teeth flashed.

"Well, I'll be. . . ." said the director, walking back to the camera position, shaking his head.

The gun battle was finally over and we started back up toward the ranchhouse where we were supposed to be living. The cameras were rolling and as I walked along, last in line, I realized that in the excitement of the moment, I still had my gun in my hand.

As we walked, I tried to shove the pistol back in my holster with authority—and missed. I tried again, and again, and couldn't find the holster in my excitement. So I stopped, grabbed the holster with my left hand, and shoved the pistol into it. "There!" I said.

All this was on the film, but the director let it go. By then, he knew he wasn't making an Oscar winner, but he must have wondered where in the world they dug up these cowboys.

Movie-making was exciting. We were allowed to sing one of our songs but we couldn't talk. We were members of the musicians union but not of AFTRA, which an actor had to belong to before he could speak on film.

CHAPTER NINE

The Blackwood Brothers

Up to this time, the Sunshine Boys had never participated in an all-night sing, which had become the thing in the gospel field. Our concerts had been either solo stands or done with a warm-up group.

We had been in Wheeling two years and all four of us were finally on our feet and making a good living.

Wally Fowler, who owned the Oak Ridge Boys and doubled as a promoter and agent for other promoters, hired us in the fall of 1951 to sing in an all-night sing in Asheville, North Carolina, one of the hot spots of gospel music. Wally supplied some talent for Riley Smith, who promoted the Asheville sings in the 3,000-seat City Auditorium.

The Statesmen were there as headliners. They were really rolling by then and under Hovie Lister's astute leadership had become one of the great quartets in the business. Some old friends of mine were singing for Hovie. Big Chief Wethering-ton of Melody Masters fame was his bass; Doy Ott, who had played piano for the Rangers and Homeland Harmony, was the baritone; Jake Hess, my former singing mate in the Sunny South Quartet, was singing the lead; and Cat Freeman, who was to become my Jonah, was Hovie's tenor. Hovie played the piano.

On the drive down from Wheeling, we determined to make the Statesmen earn their pay that night. This was the first all-night sing we'd ever taken part in, remember, and we wanted to do well.

For us, it was one of those nights in which everything fell into place. The auditorium's sound system was perfect and the house was full. Those three thousand people were right by the time we got to the stage, and we pulverized them.

We sang all of our big songs: *Dig a Little Deeper, Something Within, My God Is Real, Remember Me, Crying in the Chapel*, and Martha Carson's big hit song, *Satisfied*.

We stole the show from the Statesmen and nothing could have made us happier. Riley signed us on the spot to sing on some of his future shows, and Wally Fowler offered us a contract for $750 a week to move back to Atlanta and work for him for a year, singing three nights a week. That was $250 a night—plus record sales, which would be ours.

We didn't really want to leave Wheeling, but Atlanta was more in the center of the gospel music world and seemed to offer much more promise than West Virginia. So we accepted Wally's offer.

Something happened and Wally was unable to fulfill his contract with us, but by then it didn't matter. Word had gotten around after that Asheville show and we did not lack for bookings. We stayed busy, and folks began to consider us one of the top quartets in the business.

I bought a house on Boulevard Place in Atlanta, paid $5,500 for it. We went to Sears-Roebuck and bought furniture, not too much, just enough to get by with.

One of the items I bought was our first television set. We put it in the living room, but we hadn't bought any living room furniture. That was in 1952.

I'll never forget how long I sat on the floor watching television. When we finally bought a couch, Mary got one of those three hundred dollar jobs that was so nice she wouldn't let me sit on it and I still had to watch television from the floor.

I was watching television in the early evening hours of June 30, 1954, when word flashed on the screen that the Blackwood Brothers Quartet had had an airplane crash in Clanton, Alabama, taking the lives of R. W. Blackwood, their baritone singer, and Bill Lyles, their bass.

At that moment I had a premonition that this would affect my life. I could feel it. I didn't know why.

The Sunshine Boys and Blackwood Brothers were not particularly friendly toward each other. In fact, there had been one flare-up between us.

This occurred about three months before the airplane crash.

We heard that the Blackwoods had made some uncomplimentary remarks about us, and Ace and I sent James and R. W. Blackwood word that the next time we saw them we were going to beat the stuffing out of them. We meant it. Those were days when many still settled arguments with their fists.

We soon got our chance. There was an old trouper named Bobby Strickland who had quit the Statesmen some time before and formed his own quartet called the Crusaders Quartet.

Strickland got killed in an automobile crash while commuting between his home in Birmingham and a revival in Chattanooga. We went to his funeral.

A couple of weeks later some folks in Birmingham gave a benefit sing for Strickland's widow and two of the groups asked to participate were the Sunshine Boys and Blackwood Brothers. This was our first opportunity to follow through with our threat.

Ace and I got to the auditorium early and called James and R. W. to the back of the building where we intended to lay it to them.

"Get ready," I said, "we're fixing to collect for those things you've said about us."

Ace was going to tangle with R. W., and I was to take on James. There we stood, me six-feet-five and James five-feet-five at the most. This would have been a great battle.

R. W., who also gave away a few inches and pounds to Ace, moved quickly to save the day. "Now, boys," he said, "I'll admit that we've said some things about you, and while I'm not afraid of either of you, I can't see any reason why grown men can't sit down and settle their problems."

R. W. wasn't afraid, either. He was much of a man. And I'll have to admit that James didn't back off, even if he did look like a midget standing there bristling like a banty.

So we sat down and had a long discussion and worked things out without any fisticuffs. We all profited from that session.

When the Blackwoods had their airplane crash, they were working with the Statesmen as a team, making bookings together, traveling together, and without a doubt they formed the greatest attraction in gospel music. Where they went to sing, big crowds gathered.

After the crash, Jake Hess, who had been with the Statesmen for about four years, told James Blackwood there was only one man who could do the job on the bass for the Blackwood Brothers and that man was J. D. Sumner.

I was about the only bass who didn't apply for the job, too, because, like I said, the Blackwood Brothers and Statesmen were the best in the business and naturally would attract a lot of applications for any opening.

James called me, and I must admit that my thinking on the matter wasn't very straight. My thoughts ran along these lines: that the biggest threat to Statesmen and Blackwood Brothers' dominance of gospel singing was the Sunshine Boys, and James wanted to hire me to break up our threat and assure them of continued power. The Sunshine Boys couldn't draw people the way the Blackwoods and Statesmen could, but we could give them a fit from the stage.

I was even more amazed, though, simply because James called me after the trouble we had had a few weeks earlier.

But he did call. Mary was vacationing in Florida and I was home alone when the telephone rang.

"This is James Blackwood," he said, "of the Blackwood Brothers Quartet." I thought he was being pretty formal.

"After much prayer and thinking," he continued, "I would like to fly to Atlanta and talk with you about your coming to the Blackwood Brothers."

"Well . . ." I hedged. "I hadn't thought about coming to the Blackwood Brothers."

"I know you're happy with the Sunshine Boys," James said, "and you've got a good group, but I would like to at least come and discuss it with you."

"No," I said. "I don't believe I'm interested. I'm not interested at all."

"I don't see what it would hurt to talk about it," James said, and I could see he didn't want to give up the idea that easily.

"Well," slowly I gave in, "I don't guess it will."

The thing that suddenly turned over in my mind was that I'd get a chance to turn him down face to face.

After James hung up, I thought, *What a feather this will be in J. D. Sumner's hat! They're going to work real hard to get me and when the rest of the bass singers are trying to get the job, I'll be able to turn it down.*

I called Mary in Florida and told her about it. "You'd be crazy to leave a terrific quartet to go with those Blackwood Brothers," she said flatly.

Mary didn't even know who the Blackwood Brothers were. The business then wasn't as it later became, where groups are known coast to coast and border to border and beyond. Mary had never heard the Blackwood Brothers sing and in her eyes the Sunshine Boys were the greatest group of all.

That's the way my daddy felt, too. When I finally made up my mind to go with the Blackwood Brothers, my father thought I had pulled another stupid Sumner stunt.

At the moment, though, I was content for James to come to Atlanta. We set a date for his visit, but he wasn't satisfied to wait. He called back every day or so and sometimes, if he thought of something else he wanted to say, he'd call twice in a day.

We went on the road the week before James was supposed to fly to Atlanta on Monday, and he traced us down in Murray, Kentucky, and called me there.

He said, "J. D., I've been praying, I've been crying, I've been thinking about this thing continually, and I want you to know that money is no object. Whatever you want, I will do. I want you in the Blackwood Brothers Quartet."

After he hung up, I had my first serious thoughts about going with the Blackwood Brothers. James was awfully sincere, and he was getting through to me.

I went out and played golf and did some thinking. I had taken up golf in 1952 when I could finally afford it. I played it mostly for relaxation.

The next night—Saturday—we played Kokomo, Indiana, and when we got there early in the afternoon, Eddie and I went out to play golf. I told Eddie about things.

"You take it, J. D.," he said. "You'd be a fool if you didn't go. You can make more money with them than with any other quartet."

James called me that night as he had promised and I told him, "James, if you're willing to pay my plane fare to Memphis, I'll come there and talk with you instead of you coming to Atlanta. It's nearer for me to come there."

He agreed.

We drove from Kokomo to Louisville where I was supposed to catch a plane to Memphis. In Louisville, Ace and I got out of the car and sat down on the curb. He said he wanted to talk to me.

"George," Ace said, "I want you to go to Memphis and tell that little so-and-so that they are getting the greatest bass singer in the business."

That was the first time I had ever seen Ace Richman cry. He was a very hard man.

"I love you better than my family," Ace said. "I love you better than anybody I have ever known, and I am deeply hurt that you would do this to me, but you go on down there and don't come back. You can't afford to. This is a great opportunity."

I walked the streets of Louisville for an hour. I cried, thinking about leaving the Sunshine Boys. We had been together more than five years; we had suffered together, starved together. I remember walking by a telephone pole and knocking the stew out of it with my fist. I left the skin off my knuckles on that telephone pole, I was so emotional about leaving the Sunshine Boys.

Before I got on the airplane, I made up my mind. I would join the Blackwood Brothers Quartet.

In Memphis, I sat down with James and Doyle Blackwood, and James said: "J. D., here's what I'll do: I'll pay you either fifteen thousand a year and your expenses, or I'll give you ten thousand a year, your expenses, and a percentage of the quartet's earnings, or I'll give you an equal part of the quartet."

I didn't have to think that one over long. I said, "Well, I believe I'll just take my part of the quartet." That was instant affluence. The Blackwood Brothers were producing about a quarter-million dollars revenue every year.

That was that. Without investing a dime I became an equal member with the Blackwood Brothers.

The quartet consisted of James Blackwood singing the lead, Bill Shaw on the tenor, Cecil Blackwood, baritone, myself on the bass, and Jackie Marshall at the piano.

That November I reached my thirtieth birthday.

* * *

Johnny Atkinson replaced me with the Sunshine Boys, but didn't stay long. Then Burl Strevel took over and sang with them until he went back to the Blue Ridge Quartet.

The quartet quit using the name Sunshine Boys for a while, took the name "Diplomats," and went into pop music. That was about four years after I left and they sang pop for about ten years until 1968 when they finally quit as a full-time group.

CHAPTER TEN

The Bill Lyles Syndrome

The Blackwood Brothers were still teamed with the Statesmen when I joined them. That was the first such team in the history of quartet singing and it was a novelty. Rarely can two quartets get along well enough to work together night after night. We were never bothered by that problem, though; we liked and respected each other.

In the weeks following the airplane crash, the Blackwood Brothers drew larger crowds than ever before. Everywhere we sang, people crowded in to hear us. There were several reasons for the big crowds: some people were curious to see who had replaced Bill Lyles and R. W., and there were times that Cecil and I felt like monkeys in a cage; others came to see James and Bill Shaw and Jackie Marshall, the surviving members of the quartet; and still others turned out simply to give their support to the Blackwood Brothers following the tragedy.

We had a memorial picture album with pictures of R. W. and Bill on the cover, and we couldn't carry enough of them to sell. There were fifty in a package, and I would go out and hand a complete package to a row of people; they would open it, pass the books down, and pass the money back. I didn't know whether people paid for all the books or not, there wasn't time to count the money. It was all I could do to stuff the money in a pocket and move on to the next row.

We couldn't carry enough records, either. I doubt there was ever a time before then that a quartet made as many sales or engaged in so much emotional activity as the Blackwood Brothers during my early days with the quartet.

James paid us in cash and if he hadn't been an honest man, he could have knocked down about as much as he wanted to and we wouldn't have known the difference.

We turned all the money over to James that we collected from selling the picture albums and records. He counted it, figured up, and came back around handing fistfuls of money to each of us.

Despite all that, those were not easy times for me. Cecil, who had taken R. W.'s baritone part, didn't have it so tough because he was a Blackwood. He was R. W.'s brother. But I wasn't. I was an outsider—and I was having trouble singing the arrangements made for Bill Lyles.

My voice was an octave lower than Bill's and on the songs that he had sung so beautifully, I bombed out. On the other hand, he couldn't have touched some of the notes I was singing.

At that time, however, those things didn't matter. I had to sing what Bill had been singing. Those were the songs people wanted to hear. The problem was that Bill's songs were too high for me, and I know I didn't sound good singing them. It took almost a year for me to insert enough of my own songs into our programs for me to start sounding good.

Fort Worth, Texas, was one of the Blackwood Brothers' best towns. The first time we went there, we walked on stage and began to sing *Keys to the Kingdom*, one of the Blackwood Brothers' all-time great hit songs and one that Bill Lyles could sing beautifully.

People didn't understand the difference in the range of our voices and when we came to the bass run that went "Don't lose your keys to the Kingdom of God . . ." I could see people on the front row turning up their noses and saying, "Pshew!"

Honestly, talk about being hard to sing. And it wasn't entirely the fact that I was trying to sing Bill's arrangements, either. Everywhere we went there was animosity toward me. I could feel it. Bill Lyles was dead and he had been a popular man, and there I stood in his place, an interloper. People actually hated my guts.

Finally, when I saw those people in Fort Worth all but holding their noses while I sang, I realized I must do something about the state of affairs. So I stepped to the mike when we finished the song, and talking off the top of my head and from my heart, I said:

"Folks, I would never expect to replace Bill Lyles. He had a beautiful bass voice. James tried hard to find somebody who could match Bill's singing, but he couldn't find anybody. So he did the next best thing: He went out and hired the best-looking bass singer in the business."

Well, that cracked the ice, and it was really what helped me whip the Bill Lyles syndrome. I wouldn't have licked it in a hundred years if I hadn't begun talking to the people myself. I had never talked from stage before, but the way the people received what I said led me to believe there might be a little comedy in me.

Actually, that was the incident that led me to believe I could draw laughs on stage, and James and I began to coordinate some comedy between us. During all those years I sang with the Blackwood Brothers, I could use comedy only at James's discretion. If we were making a good hit just by singing, he wouldn't allow me to be funny. But if we reached the point where the singing wasn't getting the job done, as soon as James realized what was happening he would slip over to me and say, "Say something funny."

We kept the humor simple. I'd say something like, "Boss, it's your quartet and your program, but you need to let me sing some bass. I've had some people tell me tonight that they drove twelve miles just to hear me sing." That would always get a laugh.

When I took over the Stamps Quartet I could use comedy at my own discretion, and we made more use of it than any quartet I'd ever sung with.

After taking the bull by the horns that night in Fort Worth, I began building momentum on my own. Gradually we started changing the arrangements so I could sing as low as necessary and finally I overcame the problem of crowd hostility.

For a long while, though, Bill Lyles's wife, Ruth, didn't like me. She said the first night I went on stage to sing in Bill's place that she was sitting in the audience and if I had come up and spoken to her, she'd have popped me in the mouth. That's how much she hated me because I was standing up there in her husband's place. It was a natural reaction to tragedy. Her husband was in the grave and I was singing bass. It was a terrible time for her.

Ruth and I have grown to be close friends through the years since. She says there isn't anyone she thinks more of than me, and I am proud of it.

CHAPTER ELEVEN

On the Road
(with a Billy Goat)

When I joined the Blackwood Brothers, they had a 1951 seven-passenger Cadillac. They still owned two airplanes, a twin-engine Cessna and a single-engine Cessna, but these were grounded in Memphis and since the quartet decided not to fly again, they were soon sold.

The airplane hadn't been the best means of transportation for a gospel quartet, anyway. Oh, it would get you where you were going in the quickest possible time, which was fine, but when you got there, airports being located where they are, you were usually ten miles out of town with a P. A. system and several boxes of records to carry.

Before long, James bought a 1954 Cadillac and we used it for a year.

The first project I went to work on was the Blackwood Brothers' P. A. set. The one we had wasn't satisfactory at all, so I began bugging James for a new one. I guess I pestered him until he couldn't take it any more. One day he said, right out of the blue: "Well, go ahead and get the kind of P. A. set you want and I'll pay for it."

The one I got was one of the best, and it was the first modern, up-to-date system in our business. I bought two 77 RCA ribbon mikes, had two good speakers built, bought an RCA amplifier, and we had the best sound in the business.

That's when we went to two microphones. Until then, quartets used only one mike. We put the first tenor and the lead on one mike and the baritone and bass on the other.

* * *

There were some real characters in the Blackwood Brothers. It was a fun group.

One night we were driving from Nashville back to our homes in Memphis after an all-night sing. We were riding that 1954 Cadillac and it was Cecil's turn to drive. I was up front with him and the other three guys, James and Bill Shaw and Jackie Marshall, were asleep on the mattress in the back of the car.

We alternated by position on a long trip. The man sitting in the front seat would go straight back and sleep on the right side of the mattress. The man who had been on the right moved to the middle, the middle man to the left side, and the man on the left became the driver. The driver shifted over to the other side in the front seat.

We were going to make the trip back to Memphis without a change. Cecil said he could drive all the way easily. He said he had some thinking to do, so we all settled down and went to sleep.

Halfway home, Cecil pulled up at a truck stop.

"J. D.," he whispered, shaking me awake. "You've got to drive."

I had been sleeping soundly and came out of it slowly.

"Why?" I asked.

"My mind's hurting me," he said.

Well, that so dumbfounded me that I moved under the wheel and drove all the way to Memphis in a state of wonderment.

Cecil never offered any further explanation, and I didn't ask for one, but the thinking he had done must've been awfully heavy.

* * *

Once we were driving from Tampa to Memphis and near Tuscaloosa, Alabama, Jackie Marshall's home town, Jackie began reminiscing as he watched the familiar countryside go by.

He told us about a time when he was a kid and had a pet billy goat that he had head-butting contests with in the backyard. He vowed that he could knock the goat down and subdue it simply by butting heads.

I didn't believe him, not for a minute, and told him so.

"You've told us a lot of things, Jackie, some of which stretched the imagination pretty far, and most of which I believed, knowing you," I said, "but this time you're lying. I know you're hard-headed, but this is ridiculous. You're taking us for a bunch of idiots."

I should have dropped the subject right there, but didn't. Jackie looked hurt because I didn't believe him.

"I'll bet my head is harder than yours," I went on, about half serious.

Jackie got riled and said, "There's one way we can find out. We'll have a head-butting contest."

"Okay," I said, laughing. "As soon as we get to Memphis we'll have one."

"Don't wait till we get to Memphis," he flared. "Let's have it right here."

We had that mattress in the back of the Cadillac, spread out over an area large enough for three people to sleep on, and Jackie said we had plenty of room.

We pulled off our shoes and got on our hands and knees on opposite corners of the mattress, facing each other. The distance wasn't too great, of course, but we could shove off from the sides of the car and hit each other solidly.

It doesn't take much force to stun a fellow in a head-butting contest with Jackie Marshall. I found that out quickly.

We shoved off and collided head-on at the center of the mattress. WHAP! Man, I thought I'd been hit with a two-by-four. We backed off and Jackie was grinning. We came at each other again. BLAM! The force of the blow shook me to my toenails.

This is pretty tough, I thought, but it's as tough on him as on me. That was a good thought. It pacified me all the way back to my corner, and when I looked up and got ready to go again, Jackie wasn't grinning any more. He was laughing!

BLAM! *Blam!* blam! Each time we smashed together it was with a little less force for I was growing weaker and my head felt as if there were knots all over it.

After a half hour, Jackie must've knocked some sense into my head and I quit the contest. My knees were wobbling. I had the worst headache of my life.

"I gotta admit you've got the hardest head I ever saw," I conceded to Jackie. "I can only feel sorry for that billy goat."

A fellow knows when he's beaten in any game, and I knew he had the best of me. My head hurt for three days. I took all sorts of aspirin and Anacin and other things but nothing took away that headache. It had to wear off gradually.

If I ever die of a brain tumor, blame Jackie Marshall.

He suffered no ill effects. He had no headache. Nothing. And when I recuperated he was ready for another contest.

He couldn't goad me into another, though. When you get whipped by the champ, you know it's time to quit.

CHAPTER TWELVE

The Bus

James Blackwood is the greatest pioneer gospel music has ever had. I know there have been some great men in our business who have done a lot to make it a better field in which to work, but James Blackwood stands at the head of the list.

James has spent almost sixty years on the road, traveling in every kind of conveyance imaginable, singing the gospel. While doing this, he studied the business thoroughly and accomplished many innovations to make singing easier for everyone.

At the same time, James was receptive to new ideas from others—and that's what helped me have a field day.

Remember, James let me construct a new sound system when I joined the quartet. When I convinced him that we needed one, he encouraged me to build the best in the business.

That was the way with James: He wanted to go first class. And he wanted to innovate, to pioneer.

After he encouraged me on that sound system, I built up enough nerve to hit him with an idea that I had been toying with for some time but had never had the means to put into use.

I thought traveling by bus would be more practical than riding those limousines.

A bus would provide sleeping space, lounging space, room to get up and stretch and walk around, a large bay for storage of luggage, recordings, sound system, and whatever else, and at the same time would carry enough fuel to keep rolling. I saw no reason why quartets shouldn't travel in comfort instead of making five hundred mile trips folded up like five accordions.

I approached the quartet with the idea early in 1955 after I had been with them a few months.

"Boys, what do you think of buying a bus," I asked, "so we could all have individual compartments?"

They thought the idea was ridiculous. They laughed uproariously.

But I was sold on it and James seemed to be the type of person who was receptive to new ideas. Still, he could not comprehend that one right off.

So, I pressed the point. I must have talked nothing else for weeks. "Let's get a bus! Let's get a bus! It'll work! I know it will!" I bugged the quartet every night.

Finally, Cecil said, "Sure, let's get a bus. But I think we ought to go farther than that. We ought to get a boat, put it on the Mississippi, and when we go to St. Louis or New Orleans, why all we'll have to do is get in our boat and go."

Quickly picking up the ball, Jackie Marshall had a better idea. "We ought to get a train," he laughed. "Then we wouldn't be restricted to individual compartments. We could have a railroad car apiece."

Haw! Haw! They laughed uproariously at my expense.

By then we were riding the 1954 Cadillac, which was a comfortable car—but it hadn't been built to live in, only to ride in.

One night James was driving and I was riding in the front seat with him. The others were asleep in the rear. We talked about the bus far into the night and finally James said, "J. D., you may as well forget it. There's no way we can do it."

"Well, I know we can," I said. I had thought this one over carefully because it could involve a lot of money, and I was sure that I was right.

"It would cost too much," James said, but I was ready for him.

"I'll guarantee that I can take our car and trailer," I said, "and sell them for enough to put us on a bus."

He chewed that one over a while and finally said, "If you can do that, go ahead and do it. We'll give it a try."

That was in May of 1955. I went to Trailways the next day and looked at a 1938 model Aerocoach bus. I sold our Cadillac to Lee Roy Abernathy and our trailer to someone else and bought the bus, fixed it up inside, and had two hundred dollars left over.

Of course, the bus was old but it was air conditioned and capable of traveling.

James gave me the authority to do what was necessary to put the bus on the road. I had it cleaned and painted from one end to the other, and carpeted wall to wall. In the very back I allowed just enough room for a bed to be built across the bus. On each side, just forward of that bed, I built two bunk beds, giving us five bunks. I bought innersprings and mattresses, which turned out to be a mistake. The beds had so much spring, we couldn't sleep in them. It took a long while to figure a way around that problem.

I sectioned off the sleeping quarters and built a compartment between them and the front of the bus. There were racks for hanging our clothing, things like that.

Up front, I installed five reclining chairs, big ones in which we could lie back and sleep with our feet up. This turned out to be a stroke of fortune because when the beds proved to be too springy, we slept in the chairs, and they were more comfortable than the cramped quarters in a limousine.

For a while, everybody in the business made fun of us.

We hired a bus driver, whose name I won't mention. The boys apparently didn't trust me driving a bus.

For three months, upkeep on the bus was eleven hundred dollars a month. We put in three new clutches, and I don't remember what else.

James came to me and said, "Well, I told you we couldn't afford a bus. We can't pay out money like this and pay a driver to haul us around, too."

Our driver, I knew, had been too rough on the bus. "He's tearing it up," I told James.

James and I had our wires crossed a little right then. Having turned the bus over to me, he was thinking that the responsibility of the driver was mine, but I, knowing James was manager and boss, thought it was up to him to do something about it.

When I finally figured out our hangup, I took the bull by the horns, called up this bus driver, and fired him. "Man, you're great," I told him, "but we just can't afford you." I procrastinated a little there, but it was the easy way out.

Then I called James and told him we didn't have a bus driver any more.

"Who's going to drive us?" he asked.

"I am," I replied.

"You can't drive the bus and sing, too."

"You'll see. I'm going to prove that a bus will work."

So I became a bus driver. I had driven trucks and trailers when I was younger and I knew how to drive a heavy vehicle like a bus, but I almost killed myself. It was a hard life, driving to a place, singing, then driving on to the next, sleeping when I could.

But in the four months I drove the bus, from August to Christmas, 1955, our repair bill came to eighteen dollars. I took care of the bus, and it responded.

By that time, James and the entire Blackwood Brothers Quartet knew we could afford the bus. They knew, too, that we had something good going for us, and we all began to enjoy it. Every member of the quartet took a direct interest in it.

Cecil came to me and asked if I would teach him to drive the bus, and I did. He would take over on long, straight roads and I sat right behind him in my reclining chair. If he made a bobble, I'd wake up. Cecil became a pretty good bus driver.

But James! If there has ever been an awful bus driver, it was James.

He is a little man, to begin with, and that old steering wheel is a monster, a very large wheel, and hard to hold. The bus didn't have power steering, either, which made it that much more difficult to control.

But James, plucky as he is, gave it a whirl.

We were coming back to Memphis from South Bend, Indiana, one Sunday night and James decided he would drive. We weren't far from South Bend on a small, two-lane road when he took over. He made it fine for a while, then suddenly ran out of the road, and I'll never forget that big steering wheel, with James holding on for dear life, jerked him out of the driver's seat and walloped him against the dashboard—just WHOMP!

The Good Lord must've been riding with us that night. The bus didn't wreck—and it never did stop. James jumped back up and started wrestling the wheel until he got the bus under control again.

All that time I was lying in my chair crying. I couldn't jump on James; he was the boss.

Changing gears in a bus, you have to pull it out of low, or double low, double clutch it, and it's a synchronized movement. You have to sync it with the motor.

James wasn't a good syncher, and brother, when it came time to change gears, he'd take a good grip and Eeeeyyy-oooweee! He'd jerk it into gear. The back end of the bus would jump two feet off the ground.

The first time James changed gears I went back and told Cecil not to disturb me, that I was going to cry myself to sleep.

In time, we all learned to handle the bus reasonably well. There were a couple with whom I didn't feel entirely safe, and James, needless to say, was one of them, but they managed.

Still, I had the idea that we could afford a bus driver, if we could find one who would be safe and at the same time handle our equipment with care. There should be a way, I thought, that we could sing our concerts and get on the bus and go to sleep and forget it. That's why I wanted the bus to begin with.

Too, it was mainly up to Cecil and me to do the driving.

The next time we went to Nashville I ran across a grease monkey by the name of Bundy Brewster. He was working as a mechanic for Trailways and making forty dollars a week. Occasionally he slipped across the street to Trailblazers, another bus company, and moonlighted a little driving a bus.

Bundy assured me he could drive a bus very well, and I hired him on the spot for eighty-five dollars a week. I didn't ask James's permission or anything; I just hired him and told him to come to work the next week.

I bumped into Hovie Lister downtown and told him we were getting a driver next week.

"Is that right?" Hovie said. That's one of his favorite expressions.

"Yeah," I said, "we've got us a driver."

We were staying at the Noel Hotel in Nashville, and were to sing that night in War Memorial Auditorium, and when James came down after sleeping all day, he sat down beside me in the lobby, and I said, "James, I've hired us a bus driver."

He looked at me very straight. "Who's going to pay him?"

"Well, if we can't afford to pay him, I'll pay him, but I have got us a driver. His name is Bundy Brewster and we're paying him eighty-five dollars a week. He's coming to work next week."

As usual, James agreed to give it a try, and Bundy came on over to Memphis the following week.

His first trip was to Tupelo, Mississippi, where the Statesmen and Blackwood Brothers were singing that night.

The Statesmen got to Tupelo first and Hovie was standing in front of the auditorium waiting for us.

The auditorium in Tupelo had a large canopy over the area in front of the building to protect people from rain. You could pull up there and discharge passengers in the rain who could walk on inside the auditorium without getting wet.

Hovie was standing under the canopy waiting to get a look at this new bus driver. And on the bus, we were all sitting up front. I told Bundy to pull right on up to the front of the auditorium and we would unload the bus.

Bundy headed up toward the canopy and just kept going . . . going . . . going. . . . I was hoping all the time that he would stop. . . . I'd hate to fuss at him his first trip. . . . Then I saw Hovie running and looking back toward the bus . . . and I closed my eyes and said to myself, "Oh, no". . . and Bundy smashed into the canopy and darned near tore it off the auditorium.

Well, I want you to know that I suffered some humiliation. All the Blackwood Brothers got up, glared at me—not at Bundy—and silently filed off the bus.

When I got up enough nerve to get off, Hovie was standing there grinning like the cat who swallowed the canary, and the only thing he said was, "Terrific bus driver you got there, John. Terrific!"

I didn't say anything and he walked off.

But I knew right then that Bundy had a few things to learn about driving a bus.

He learned well, though, and stayed with the Blackwood Brothers many years, becoming the oldest bus driver in gospel singing in length of service. Bundy also learned to operate the sound system and when the Blackwood Brothers were on stage, he knew exactly how to control the sound for every song they did.

*   *   *

For several months after we went aboard the bus, the Statesmen continued to ride in their Cadillac limousine, pulling a little trailer loaded with records and such.

Leaving a place, they would jump in their car and head for our next date, zipping out of town while we steered that cumbersome old bus toward the city limits. By the time we got her wound up and on the open road, they were long gone.

We couldn't keep up with them, of course; they were at least twenty-five miles an hour faster, but ours was a steady gait. We carried a hundred twenty-five gallons of fuel, had a rest room on the bus, and didn't have to stop for anything.

In a trip of three or four hundred miles, the Statesmen would beat us by forty-five minutes, and Jake Hess would make it a point to check into the hotel quickly and stay up to see what time we arrived. He'd put on a big show about how long they'd been there and how rested he was. When I came in, he'd be waving at me like he'd been there a day and a half.

"A bus is just not practical, George," Jake would tell me. "Oh, if you had two or three thousand miles to go, it might be different, but for two or three hundred miles, they just won't get the job done."

By this time the Blackwood Brothers and Statesmen had started some publishing companies. I was running ours and Jake was in charge of theirs. We thought we had reached a point where we needed to discuss things at night. We would get together and have our big business discussions the same as James and Hovie.

But I got fed up with Jake and his ridicule of our bus. We were getting to be proud of that bus.

One night in Little Rock, I went to Jake and said, "How about riding with me tonight. I want to talk to you about some things."

"Aw, I don't want to ride that stupid bus," he said.

"It's important, Jake," I said. "I need to talk to you."

"Well, if it's important. . . ." he gave in.

When I got him on the bus, however, I waited until the Statesmen had left in their limousine, and then I told him I didn't have anything to talk about. I made him sit in my chair, covered him with a blanket, put a pillow behind his head, and said, "Now, go to sleep and I'll see you in Fort Worth. I want you to see how it is to ride the right way."

Jake went to sleep leaving Little Rock and I woke him in front of the Texas Hotel in Fort Worth.

The first thing he said was, "We're gonna buy a bus."

Jake went right in to the grill where Hovie was having breakfast. He had been there about forty-five minutes. I stayed in the lobby, but at a point from where I could see them. Jake went straight up to Hovie and they had a serious conversation.

In a few minutes Hovie came out, walked directly up to me and asked, "Where can we get a bus?" He was so direct and he and Jake had talked so little that I think they had probably discussed the matter before.

I got on the telephone and called the Greyhound people in Dallas. They priced a pair of Silversides for $5,000 each. So I went to James and talked to him about the Blackwood Brothers getting a new bus, too.

James agreed, and the Blackwood Brothers and Statesmen bought twin Silverside buses. The Statesmen were the second group to own and travel in a bus. Within a few short years, every professional group in gospel singing, most of the country and western outfits, and most of the rock groups traveled by private coach. Today, you can hardly drive any distance without passing an entertainment group of some sort riding down the road in their bus. When we pass some of those groups I can hardly resist the temptation to laugh and think: There may go some of the fellows who laughed so hard at me back in 1955.

James and Hovie asked me to fix up both of our new Silversides. I had chairs built according to each man's height this time. I learned that lesson on the first bus, because I was so much longer than most of the other guys.

As soon as we got those new buses on the road we discovered the secret of sleeping aboard in bunks. We had had so much trouble with the beds on that first bus that I didn't have any built in the new ones. Before the inside of the Blackwood Brothers' bus was completed, we had to use it for a trip, so I took the mattresses off our old bus—they were practically unused—and threw them on the floor of the new Silverside.

A couple of us stretched out on the mattresses after we got underway and discovered that we could sleep fine. We didn't bounce or roll or anything.

I slept like a doll and when I awoke it dawned on me that the innersprings had been the source of our sleeping troubles. The bus springs themselves gave us all the flexibility we needed, and when we tried to sleep on innersprings, it was like sleeping on two sets of springs that gave with each bounce of the bus.

Afterward, I added bunks to each of the new buses, building hard-bottomed beds with plyboard. When we began riding the new buses permanently, we started using the beds.

We kept those buses until 1962 when both the Blackwood Brothers and Statesmen bought brand new buses. We had them custom built inside, putting in private compartments for each man for the first time. We could each get into our own bunks, close the doors and have some privacy. Each bunk had its own light.

These buses cost $41,000 each, but by the time we got the insides custom built, equipped them with tires, and figured up the whole bill, they ran right at $47,000 each.

From that day on, we rode in style.

CHAPTER THIRTEEN

Traveling Men

Traveling and singing are the two big workaday items in the life of a quartet man—and the Blackwood Brothers got plenty of both.

With the Sunny South Quartet, travel was limited. We had two radio programs daily, at 7 a.m. and noon, and in those days there was no way to transcribe our radio shows, so we couldn't go far to singing engagements. We were restricted more or less to the bounds of Florida, and seldom did we reach the ends of that state.

The Sunshine Boys traveled more, but not while we were in Wheeling. We had to sing daily on WWVA and drive to our concerts, which put something of a mileage restriction on us. But by then, we could transcribe a couple of programs and take longer trips, like the one to Asheville when we tore up the Statesmen and got the big break.

In Atlanta, the Sunshine Boys traveled much more, but nothing I'd done compared with the travel the Blackwood Brothers racked up, especially after we began riding the bus.

In 1956, James made some bookings in the Los Angeles area and the Blackwood Brothers pioneered professional gospel singing on the West Coast.

The Blackwood Brothers company paid all expenses and we took our wives and children, drove our own cars, and made something of a holiday out of a business trip. We enjoyed ourselves tremendously, but didn't make expenses. Still, pioneer that he was, James made future bookings in Long Beach and other places around Southern California. His foresight was correct. We made twelve hundred dollars on our second trip to Los Angeles. Only the quartet made that second trip, and we rode the bus.

From there it was amazing how fast gospel music grew on the West Coast. The Blackwood Brothers then pioneered the Oakland area, and finally Seattle, and the reception was the same in those places, slow at the start but gradually improving until it paid off handsomely.

Adoption of the bus for travel enabled quartets to make extended trips of two, three, and four weeks. Such travel in automobiles would be killing, but we could relax on the bus, especially having our own driver.

Before I had been with the Blackwood Brothers very long, we were singing in California, all over the northeast, midwest, southwest, and then through Canada.

Both the open road and the stage presented challenges—and we met them head-on.

That first bus itself was a challenge. We broke down in Texas in the middle of the night, somewhere between Houston and Fort Worth. We were way out in the middle of nowhere, on one of the loneliest stretches of highway you'll ever see.

Ronnie Blackwood, one of R. W.'s sons, was traveling with us that summer. He was just a kid.

All the other guys were asleep except for Ronnie and me. Ronnie was under the bus, lying on his back, working on something, and grease had dropped all over his face. He had it on his hands, his face, all over him.

He probably felt I was giving him a bad time, and our tempers were growing short. We were getting madder by the minute at that bus.

I crawled up under the bus and said something to Ronnie, and he reached up, got a whole handful of that black grease, and smeared it across my face.

Before I could grab him, he slipped out from under the bus and took off. So did I. It's a good thing I didn't catch him, because I would have wrung his neck, but James said it was kind of weird, waking up in the middle of the night out on the Texas plains, hearing a couple of nuts screaming like wild Indians. He thought he was under attack, but when he looked out the window to see what was going on, he watched me

chase Ronnie over the horizon. We must have looked like Wile
E. Coyote chasing the roadrunner.

*   *   *

We sang one night in Lubbock, Texas, and then got on that
old bus and headed for Fort Worth. The Rebels were on the
program with us and were thinking about buying a bus. London Parris, the Rebels' bass singer, rode with us that night so
I could teach him to drive the bus.

We all had our clothes hung on a big rack back in the bus,
and luggage was scattered around.

London was driving and doing very well, until he came to a
small town. In a lot of those tiny Texas towns, drainage systems
weren't what they should have been. Most of their drainage was
through ditches along the roadsides, and when those ditches
crossed the road, they crossed on top of it. There weren't any
culverts under the road. So, at most intersections there was a
sharp, sudden dip, like a speed breaker turned upside down.

Late that night London bore down on one of those towns at
a pretty good clip. He roared through an intersection, hit one
of those dips, and for a quarter of a mile that bus looked like a
bucking bronco going sixty miles an hour.

It threw every one of us out of our reclining chairs into the
aisle, and brought all our clothes down on top of us.

Thank the Lord, London afterward learned to drive a bus a
little better. He later sang with the Blackwood Brothers and took
an occasional turn at the wheel on some of the longer trips.

*   *   *

The worst scare I ever got in a bus was late one night in that
rolling country just south of Durham, North Carolina.

We had sold our original bus to the Rebels and were riding
in the Silverside. The Rebels in turn had ridden our old bus for
a while, then sold it to the Harvesters Quartet in Charlotte,
North Carolina. The Harvesters also used it for a time, then
bought a better one and had the old one parked in Charlotte.
They hadn't been able to sell it. I guess that one bus initiated
more quartets to bus travel than any other vehicle. Somebody is
probably using it today.

Anyway, we had sung in Charlotte that night and were heading for Harrisburg, Pennsylvania, for a date the next night.

Everybody had rolled into bed after a long night in Charlotte, and in the wee hours of the morning Bundy approached Durham. About fifteen miles south of the city he drove down a long hill and started up another one equally as tall.

Near the top of the hill, the driveshaft fell out of the bus with a loud CLUNK! On the way out, it struck and punctured the diaphragm on the air brakes.

The bus didn't quite make it to the top of the hill, where Bundy intended to ditch it if nothing else. It rolled to a halt short of the top, then began to move backward down the hill, gathering momentum.

With the driveshaft gone, Bundy had no gears and couldn't control the bus that way; with the diaphragm punctured, he had no brakes and couldn't stop it, either.

So he did the next thing that came to mind.

"J. D.!" he screamed at the top of his voice, blasting me out of bed.

I ran forward in my underwear, and saw that we were rolling backward.

"What's going on?" I asked.

"I can't stop the bus," Bundy shouted.

"What do you mean, you can't stop the bus? Put on the brakes."

"I don't have any brakes."

"Put it in gear."

"Don't have any gears, either."

"Let me have it," I yelled, and Bundy bailed out. I slid into the driver's seat and the only thing left to do was guide the bus the best I could, trying to hold it in the road. I prayed no cars would come over the hill behind us.

We hit bottom at a pretty good clip and started backward up the other hill. The bus slowed going up that hill and the other guys should have jumped, but they stayed with us.

Then the bus rolled forward, down into the valley, up the other hill, stopped, went backward again, down into the valley, up the rear hill. It seemed we see-sawed that way, up and down, for half an hour, the arcs growing shorter each time, until finally we came to a halt down in the valley.

Sweat was rolling off my brow in rivulets. There was a loud collective sigh of relief when we came to a stop.

I caught a ride into Durham and sent a wrecker back for

the bus. Meanwhile, knowing we needed transportation on to Pennsylvania, I called the Harvesters in Charlotte and borrowed our old bus. They got a driver to bring it to Durham where we piled in it, leaving Bundy behind with our bus, and headed for Harrisburg.

I was driving about a hundred miles north of Durham when the motor suddenly gave way with a loud THUNK! It threw a rod right through the block. Eventually it cost us seven hundred fifty-two dollars to replace that engine, but at the time that wasn't our foremost problem. We still had to get to Harrisburg, and here we were stuck again in the middle of nowhere.

Together we walked to a little country store to try to hire someone to drive us to the nearest town, Petersburg, Virginia, where we might rent a couple of cars. By this time, most of the guys were glaring at me because I was the one responsible for us being on a bus in the first place.

We talked one man into driving some of us to Petersburg for fifteen dollars, but he said he wouldn't take all five, that we'd have to get somebody else to haul a couple of us.

Wally Varner, who had replaced Jackie Marshall at the piano, and I stayed behind to ask another man to drive us to Petersburg.

"What'll you take us to Petersburg for?" I asked him.

"Fifteen dollars," he said.

I was a little burned because the other guy wouldn't take us all, so I said, "Okay, we'll give you twenty-five."

He thought he had struck such a good deal that he almost beat the other car to town.

In Petersburg we rented a car and drove to Harrisburg. We got to the auditorium at intermission, went on stage, sang for an hour, then checked into a hotel and went to bed.

Bundy got there about 3 a.m. in our bus, which had been repaired in quick time, and in the morning we loaded up, turned in our rented car, and went on to our next engagement.

*   *   *

In every quartet someone has to be in charge of the bus, and with the Blackwood Brothers it was me. Keeping up a bus will keep a man on his toes under the best of conditions. Soon after we got the new Silverside, the Blackwood

Brothers went to Denver, Colorado, for two weeks of revival at Calvary Temple.

It was September, the sun was shining beautifully, and it wasn't cold. In fact, it was so warm when we pulled into Denver that I hadn't even thought about checking the antifreeze.

We parked at the church and checked into a hotel. During the next two weeks we were so wrapped up in the revival and in our singing that I neglected even to think about antifreeze.

One night it snowed. Then the temperature dropped to 5 below zero.

At the end of the revival, we loaded up the bus and prepared to move out. The bus was hard to start, but we finally got it going and when we started down the street, you wouldn't believe the amount of water that came out of all sides of the motor. It burst wide open.

All the water ran out in the space of a couple of miles. We took the bus to a garage and spent two or three hundred dollars trying to patch it up, but in the end we had to install a new motor. My mistake cost us a pretty penny there.

Next time we came to Calvary Temple in Denver, I was presented with a plaque, making me mechanic-of-the-year. It had a wrench engraved on it.

It was all in fun, of course; they were really hep at that church.

*   *   *

In all the time Bundy drove us while I was with the Blackwood Brothers and in charge of the bus, I had to jump on him with both feet only once.

We were running in tandem one night toward Detroit, the Blackwood Brothers and Statesmen. O'Neil Terry was driving the Statesmen and Bundy was driving us.

O'Neil was in front and going at a pretty good clip when he came upon a road block. He didn't see it in time to stop and crashed through it. Fortunately, the bus didn't wreck and no one was injured.

Bundy, running close behind the Statesmen, saw O'Neil go through the road block and crammed on our brakes in time to come to a screeching stop right up next to the obstacle.

The Statesmen backed out and got straightened up again and headed on toward Detroit. All that time, and while we checked into a hotel and went to bed, I thought about our near-miss with that road block.

I got up early in the afternoon the next day and it was still on my mind.

We sang that night in Detroit, slept at the hotel again, and early the next morning we were to leave for California, going by way of El Paso, Texas, where we had a booking en route.

By the time I was ready to leave, I knew what had to be done. Our bus drivers were getting careless and it was time to straighten out the situation and bring things under control. Bundy was my responsibility and I intended to make him more conscious of his own responsibilities.

I went to breakfast in the coffee shop and sat down beside Bundy. I ordered coffee.

Bundy was his old, amazing self that morning . . . "Good morning, Mr. Sumner" . . . and all that jazz.

"Good morning, Bundy," I said. "I've got some bad news for you," coming quickly to the point.

"What's that?"

"You're fired."

Just like that. It shook him.

"How come I'm fired?" he asked.

"Well, to begin with," I said, "you don't know how to drive. You've got no idea how to drive a bus."

"I thought I was doing good."

"Well, you haven't been doing good. You've been getting more reckless every day. You have the lives of the Blackwood Brothers Quartet at stake—and you're fired."

Bundy could hardly believe it. He had grown to love driving us around, and he became very despondent.

"Tell you what," I finished. "You work the next two weeks since we've already started this trip. But after that, Bundy, you've had it."

That was the first part of my plan, to let it soak into Bundy's head that we weren't satisfied with his driving and intended to do something about it.

Before I left my hotel room, I put the second part of my

plan into operation. I took one of the hotel's water glasses, just an ordinary water glass, and put it in my brief case. At that time one of the things a man of importance carried was a brief case; if you didn't have one, you were nothing.

As I walked out of the hotel that morning, my impressive-looking brief case contained only that one object: a stolen water glass. But it became a most important item, and was perhaps worth the price even of theft.

On the bus we had a tank of water that fed through a spigot into a sink. I made a point of being the last aboard the bus. All the other guys were sitting up front, well rested, looking forward to an early-morning ride.

I went straight to the sink, took the glass out of the brief case, and filled it with water. I went back up front and set the glass of water on the bus's flat dashboard.

That had everybody's attention.

"What's that for?" Bundy asked.

I said, "Bundy, that glass of water may save your job. In two weeks I'm going to hire another bus driver, and if you think you can learn to drive this bus well enough to protect our lives, I'll consider re-hiring you."

"What's that got to do with a glass of water?" he asked.

There's where I started running my bluff. I had heard that Greyhound used a water glass system to teach its drivers how to handle a bus so easily that little old ladies in the aisle wouldn't fall down every time they turned a curve or shifted a gear.

"You take my seat," I told Bundy. "I'm going to drive this bus three hundred miles without spilling a drop of this water."

The fellows were listening by that time, and I saw a grin or two among them, evidence that I was opening my big mouth again and positioning my foot in front of it. They didn't know about my little discussion with Bundy and were wondering what was going on.

Bundy sat in my chair behind the driver's seat. I didn't know whether I could get out of Detroit with that glass of water still sitting there, because I didn't really think I was that good a driver, but it was worth the risk of Bundy's finding out.

I drove very carefully, very softly, like a man sitting on a crate of eggs.

For three hundred miles I talked to Bundy about how he could be the new bus driver, succeeding himself, if he wanted the job, which he did, of course, very badly. I gave him all the little tips I had learned driving on the open road, and he absorbed what I said. I like to think that I helped him. The others were listening, too.

At any rate, three hundred miles down the road, I pulled over and stopped. I hadn't spilled a drop of water.

Bundy took over and drove a couple of hundred miles with one eye on the road and the other on that water glass. He drove until he was so sleepy he couldn't go any farther, then called Cecil.

Cecil had been watching the water glass, too, and like Bundy, he drove very carefully, determined not to spill any of it.

We switched off like that on the 1,700-mile drive from Detroit to El Paso, and that water glass made cautious drivers out of all of us.

Bundy was driving the last stage toward El Paso when he became sleepy again. The rest of us were in our bunks asleep, so Bundy stopped, woke Cecil, and crawled into his bunk as Cecil took the wheel.

Cecil rolled that bus into El Paso, keeping a sharp eye on the glass of water, which had become a fetish for us. Cecil was determined not to be the one who spilled the water.

But fate lay in wait down the street. And when fate stepped in, it landed with both feet.

Three inebriated Mexican men were parked on the side of a street and as Cecil approached, they suddenly decided to make a U turn and go back the other way.

The driver of the car didn't bother to look back. He cranked up the engine, slipped the car into gear, and pulled broadside into the street just as Cecil came rolling down upon him in that big bus.

SMASH!!!

Cecil hit them broadside at about forty miles an hour. There was no way he could have stopped the bus; the accident was later ruled unavoidable. But that didn't help the Mexicans.

Their car was knocked slap out of the street and over onto the lawn of a motel.

The car was demolished. The three men were cut and bleeding, and two were knocked clean out of the car, and one all the way out of the street and onto the lawn of the motel.

When the bus came to a halt, all of us in the back were in that stupid limbo one experiences when literally jerked from the depths of sleep.

And Cecil, not knowing whether he had killed the Mexicans, or battered our bus beyond going, didn't take time to get off and find out.

He came flying back through the bus, almost hysterical.

"J. D.," he screamed. "J. D.!"

"What? What?" I grabbed him by the shoulders. "What's the matter, Cecil?"

"J. D.," he sobbed, tears streaming down his cheeks, "I spilled that glass of water!"

The Mexicans were lying out there in and around the street, cut and bleeding, but apparently they were limber enough from tequila that they weren't hurt too much. At least they never did anything about the wreck; we never heard from it one way or the other. Probably we should have because, after all, we hit them, even if they did pull out in front of us. I think they knew it was their fault, so they just let it drop.

The wreck banged up the front of the bus a little and ruined the door. We had to buy a new door, but we were in a hurry and when we saw the Mexicans weren't badly hurt and the police ruled the accident unavoidable we took the bus and went on. We didn't try to collect from the Mexicans, we just paid for the door ourselves.

We made the rest of the trip with that banged-up door on the bus, the wind whistling a tune through it, and we didn't miss a date.

But if we thought that bus, because of the wrecked door, was airy, it was nothing to one ride we made sometime later. We were going to Atlanta and some kind of bird, a crow, I think, hit us head-on and broke out the right windshield.

I was driving, doing about fifty when the bird hit us, and all the other guys were lying back in their beds. When the windshield was smashed the air came through that bus with such a rush the cover rose off their beds and flew into the back of the bus.

That was one more cold, airy ride.

CHAPTER FOURTEEN

Companions All

Compatibility is as important to a quartet as singing ability. If five guys can't get along with each other and have some fun together, they may as well disband and look for some other kind of work.

I've been fortunate in always being able to sing with people I liked.

I've said a lot about James Blackwood in this book, and I feel that our readers will get a pretty good picture of him— or at least of how I feel about him. But what of the other guys?

Take Cecil, a nice, easy-going guy; I was never in an argument with Cecil. Never even a little riff in the eleven years we sang together, nor even since I left the Blackwood Brothers.

There was never even a hard word between the two of us and that's pretty darned rare, especially when I'm one of the people, because I doubt that I'm the easiest man in the world to get along with.

James and I had two run-ins, pretty good ones, too, but Cecil and I, never a one.

The man who couldn't get along with Cecil Blackwood had problems. Cecil carried his share of the load, never complained about it, and worked for the good of the company and his fellowman. That made him a hundred percent in my book.

Never had any trouble with Bill Shaw, either, but Bill's a peculiar person. He's a loner. He just never did buddy around. He was always off by himself and never got close enough to anyone in the quartet to be called a buddy.

Many artists—and I'm speaking of singers as artists—are that way. Most talented people are a little stand-offish.

We never knew where Bill would be at any time. We'd set a time to go and nobody would have seen Bill for a couple of hours and we'd think sure as the world we were going to have to leave him this time, and just about the time we'd have to crank up the bus and go, Bill would come around the corner.

I remember taking a walk with Bill one day in a strange city, just to pass the time before a singing that night. We were talking, just walking down the street, and I turned around to say something to him and discovered I was talking to myself. He was gone.

That happened other times, too. He'd just take off down the street, walking fast, or see something he wanted to look at around a corner, and suddenly you'd be walking alone and talking to yourself and everybody looking at you like you were a fool.

Bill was the strangest person I was ever around about such stuff as that.

But I don't believe there was anybody in the business who could touch Bill Shaw when he really decided to sing tenor. I was listening to one of the Blackwood Brothers' old records the other day and he sang as well on that record as anybody I ever heard.

Sometimes Bill went on stage and seemed not to care how he sounded, but he evermore cared when he got in a recording studio.

He was a great singer. Likeable person, too, despite that quality of aloofness.

*   *   *

I don't think there has ever been anyone in our business who could play more piano than Wally Varner and Jackie Marshall.

James came over to my house one Christmas and we pulled out a stack of old Blackwood Brothers records that we hadn't heard in some time. I've made a collection of records; got every record we ever made, and I keep them back until I want to reminisce a little, then I pull them out and put them on the stereo.

Well, James came over for breakfast a day or two before

Christmas and I put on a bunch of records that James hadn't heard for a while and Wally was playing the piano on them.

We sat there like two guys amazed, like a couple of kids who'd never heard Wally Varner play a piano before.

When Wally Varner played the piano for a quartet there wasn't room for any other instrument. He filled every hole and every crack.

Today you need other instruments, but you didn't need them when Wally was around. Man, that beat all I ever heard. Even though I sang seven or eight years with Wally at the keyboard, I still couldn't believe the difference when I sat there listening to those records.

It's hard to believe there were piano players like Wally and Jackie, because for a long while after them, piano players played session music. They even played it in the programs.

There wasn't a nicer guy to get along with than Wally, either. Always cutting up. Nice guy to ride down the highway with. A real buddy.

He always kept you laughing.

Jackie was a great piano player, but he didn't have Wally's temperament. I guess Wally got tempered back in those days of automobile riding with the Homeland Harmony and Rangers quartets. But Jackie was always like a kid.

Jackie was a better salesman than Wally, and probably played more piano. He was a classical pianist. But when you got down to it, Wally contributed more to the singing and Jackie more to the show. Jackie would sometimes put in so much piano that we had to wait for him to get through. Wally did nothing but add to, and when it came to Jack Marshall going out to play the piano he put in more showmanship, piano, style, more action than anybody I've ever sung with.

Today you've got two different styles. You've got Anthony Burger who played with the Kingsmen. I would have to say that he is the best piano player in the business, but he is not the best in the business to play for a quartet.

C. J. Almgren, who plays for the Stamps Quartet, cannot play what Anthony does, but he can add more to a quartet. A man who knows music knows that C. J. is putting in exactly what it takes for this quartet to perform classy singing. Anthony Burger can put in so much piano—and it's every bit great—until it takes away from the quartet's singing. He's a classical pianist and he evermore proves it on every song. I want to emphasize that the kid is evermore fantastic, but when I choose a piano player I like one who does not distract from the singing.

The difference in Anthony and C. J. is the same difference we used to have between Wally and Jackie.

We don't use only the piano in the Stamps Quartet. C. J. plays the Ensoniq. He can program it—it's done with computer chips made by real instruments—and orchestrate a whole song on stage exactly like we recorded it. It's not like using tracks. In *God Shall Wipe Away All Tears* we have a place where we slow the song down, and C. J. can slow that Ensoniq down right with us. Here's another thing of value about it: There is one quartet now—and the Stamps used to be guilty of the same thing—that has so many instruments they destroy the singing of the quartet. Sometimes that's good because the instruments cover poor singing. But you can control how loud and how fast or slow the Ensoniq goes. It used to be that our musicians would turn up their instruments so loud that people would tell us afterward, "We enjoyed you, but we couldn't hear you." Then I would go to the musicians and say, "Cut down the amplifier. Don't play so loud," and they would get mad and wouldn't play at all. The Ensoniq is the way to go when you don't have a man in the audience controlling sound.

*   *   *

Jackie Marshall is a millionaire today. So's Wally Varner. But when Jackie was playing piano for the Blackwood Brothers, he was still struggling along.

Jackie had two personalities, or maybe it was just one that sometimes split, but he'd want to fight you one minute and be telling you how much he loved you the next.

When I went with the Blackwood Brothers, we had a company car and when it broke down, we'd use either my Cadillac or James's Lincoln. Jack had a little one-seater coupe and Bill Shaw had a Ford, so ours were the only two spare cars we could use on the road.

We'd take it turn about, James and me. We'd take my car one time when the company car broke down, and next time we'd take his. We didn't make any business arrangements; the company, which was the Blackwood Brothers organization, would buy the gas and oil and that was it.

I took my car on a long trip once and came up with the idea of the company paying James and me ten cents a mile for using our cars because we were tearing them up.

If all five of us had had cars that we could use and we had been taking turn about, I wouldn't have complained, but since it was only James's and mine, I sounded off about it.

We were in Greenville, South Carolina, and I passed a few remarks to Jackie, needling him, about how his old car wasn't fit to go and I wasn't going to tear up my car for the company any more, and I agitated him just enough until he told me:

"If you open your mouth one more time about my car, J. D., I'll whip you."

"Whip me?" I said. "You can't whip me." He was a foot shorter and a whole lot lighter than me.

"I know I can't whip you," he shouted, "but I'll whip you anyway."

Well, now, I didn't know whether I was capable of coping with logic like that—and, too, I remembered the billy goat— so I let the subject drop while we were both ahead.

*   *   *

We had great rapport in the Sunshine Boys, too. Got along like four brothers, except maybe we didn't fight and argue as much as brothers do.

Ace Richman was the type of person who loved very few people. He was a hard guy. If Ace liked you or if you worked with him, he evermore would look out for you. He would see that you and your family didn't do without.

I guess I got under Ace's skin as much as anybody who ever worked with him; at least, he told me I did. But he told me he loved me as much as he loved his wife and children. He told me that when I started to go with the Blackwood Brothers.

I don't believe you could find a better man than Ace Richman in keeping his word. If he told you he would do something, you didn't need it in writing. He was as good at his word as any man I've ever known.

* * *

Freddie Daniels was always easy to get along with, but he was a cocky little fellow in his younger days.

Oh, he'd fuss with you. I'll never forget the day we were singing over WWVA in Wheeling when we got into an argument about how Freddie sang his part.

He always thought he sang an octave high, but he really sang alto, the way our music was written. I told him he sang his part in the same place a lady did, but because he was a man it sounded higher.

The late, great Lee Roy Abernathy verified the fact. I don't remember where we discussed it with Lee Roy, who had been *the* professor of gospel music for many years, and Lee Roy agreed that Freddie sang it the way it was written, not an octave higher.

You see, in a lady's quartet, the alto sings the music where it's written, the soprano sings it where it's written, the tenor sings an octave high, making her the highest singer in the group, and the lady bass usually raises it an octave.

In a male quartet, the first tenor, which is the same as alto in a lady's quartet, sings the music where it's written; the lead, which corresponds to soprano, sings an octave low; baritone sings it where it's written, and the bass ranges according to how low he can sing.

Ace and Eddie also agreed with Lee Roy and me that Freddie sang tenor just where it was written, and when the discussion came to a head we were standing around the mike in the studio, about to go on the air, and I gigged Freddie so hard, I guess, that he threw a song book at me and hit me in the face with it.

I grabbed him and started to punch him in the mouth, but about that time the light came on and Ace punched me in the ribs and I hit the theme song as Eddie gave the piano roll, and we sang *Going Home Some Day to Be with Jesus*.

During the first break in the program, I told Freddie, "Fat boy, I'm going to whip you when this is over," but when we finished the program we were already laughing about it and our spat was over.

Freddie and I were very close. We were the kind who could take our families on trips together and get along.

He was a lot like me back then, though—a little fiery.

But he still sings his part where it's written.

                    *   *   *

Eddie Wallace was the quiet guy. He was the easy-going type. You'd never have a fuss with Eddie. He'd agree with you. Anything you said, didn't matter what, Eddie would agree with you.

He was a funny guy on stage—very, very funny.

And he was a nice guy to work with. I don't think I need say any more than that about Eddie: He was a nice guy to work with.

CHAPTER FIFTEEN

On Stage

Those were great years with the Blackwood Brothers. We were at the top, one of the two best drawing cards in gospel singing. I was singing lower than anyone in the business and James, Cecil, and Bill Shaw were the perfect trio to sing with. Their range was so high and so beautifully smooth that I could sing as low as I wanted and never have to worry about being out of blend.

We had some big songs. When I first came on the scene with the Blackwoods, their big songs were carryovers from the days before Bill Lyles and R. W. were killed: *The Man Upstairs, Keys to the Kingdom, How About Your Heart*, and others like that.

Then I started putting some songs into our repertoire: *The Old Country Church; God Made a Way; Inside the Gate; When I'm Alone; Keep Me; Something Old, Something New*, and we changed our style of singing.

We had many hit songs in the gospel field during those years. And I learned a lot about singing.

I learned some of the rudiments of comedy, too. I learned how to talk on stage, and felt that I was becoming a well-rounded stage personality. I was usually the straight man for James's jokes, but he also encouraged me to try some comedy of my own from the stage. So on occasion I would play the village idiot, which at times didn't come hard.

That's the role I was playing in Little Rock, Arkansas, one evening when I made the biggest goof I ever made on stage.

I stepped to the mike during our part of the program to do my elevator routine which always drew a laugh.

The routine went like this:

"James," I would begin, "do you know what happened to me in the hotel this afternoon?"

"No," James would say. "Tell us."

"Well, I went out to the elevator and rang the bell and when the elevator came up to my floor, there was a new girl running it.

"I got on and said, 'Lobby, please,' and she said, 'Thank you,' closed the door, took hold of the handle and pushed it all the way over, and down we went—ZZzzzOOOOOO-mmmmmm!!!!!

"We hit bottom with a thud and the elevator girl, hearing me groan, turned around and said, 'What's the matter, mister, did we stop too quick?' And I answered, 'Oh, no, I always wear my britches down around my ankles.'"

But this night in Little Rock, the gremlins hit me just as the elevator was going down, and when we hit the bottom with a thud, I heard her groan and turned to her and said, "What's the matter, did we stop too quick?" And she said, "Oh, no, I always wear my britches down around my ankles."

You should have heard that audience howl. I didn't realize I'd gotten the story backward, but I had never heard a crowd break up that way over that joke.

I turned to James and asked, "What did I say?"

"You fool," he said, laughing as hard as he could. "You've got *her* britches down instead of yours."

That one really embarrassed me.

* * *

I got a good laugh in Long Beach, California, at Big Chief's expense the night in 1963 that we cut our *On Stage* album before a live audience. Personally, I think that was perhaps the best album the Blackwood Brothers ever recorded.

When we recorded before an audience like that, we had a man on each side of the stage directing applause. They started the applause and stopped it, controlling the applause to fit the recording.

On that night, Big Chief was on the left side of the stage directing applause.

We were singing *He Means All the World to Me*, a song I

had written, and when I started to go down real low, a baby cried in the audience.

I paused in mid-note and said, "Bless its heart," purely by instinct, and the audience laughed, and I went on and finished the song.

When I got through and backed up from the mike, the audience was applauding loudly because I had been down so low. Big Chief came over to me and stuck out his hand and said, "You'd better hope they heard that baby cry. If it's not on the record, you've made a fool out of yourself."

"I know it's on the record," I said. "There're mikes in the audience."

Great showman that he is, James realized that we had a hit on our hands, and when he saw Big Chief shake my hand, his trigger-quick mind capitalized on the incident.

"Well, now, there's something," he said into the mike— and all this is on the record. "Big Chief coming out and congratulating him. That's really something, one bass singer complimenting another."

Then I had a brainstorm. I went to the mike and said, "Naw, when I said 'Bless its heart,' I thought I heard a baby crying; it was Big Chief."

That brought down the house in laughter.

Even now, people come up to me and request that song, but they don't remember its name. They'll say, "Sing the song where the baby cried."

*   *   *

Remember I said Cat Freeman was my Jonah? He had a way of tearing me up on stage. Cat sang tenor for the Statesmen a few years before Denver Crumpler joined Hovie's quartet, and he and I used to try to get each other's goat.

There were times when a program began to drag that James would bring me to the mike to do a skit. I had two or three things that usually put the audience in a better mood, things like the elevator routine, but that one could only be used in cities large enough to have a hotel several stories high.

We were working in an old cow barn in South Georgia one night when James called on me. The place was built so that from the stage you could see only that part of the audience directly in front of you. You couldn't see a thing beneath the balcony.

I was doing my Sad Sam Jones routine about a Negro preacher making his announcements in church and when I got to a part that was serious, not at all funny, someone back there under the balcony would fall out of his seat laughing.

That clown was so funny that everybody in the house got to laughing at him.

When I came to a part that should have been funny, he wouldn't crack a grin.

He completely took the audience away from me. I couldn't make the crowd do a thing. I would give a punch line and the people would wait and see if this guy was going to laugh. If he didn't, they didn't. When I'd hit a serious part, he'd have himself a belly laugh and get up and walk around hee-hawing and holding his stomach. He tore that audience up.

Toward the last of the skit, I recognized him. It was Cat Freeman who was then singing tenor for the Statesmen. I should have known who it was, and I decided right then that I would pay him back.

The next night we were working a Christmas party in Brewton, Alabama, and before the show I went to Hovie and told him I wanted him to put Cat on for a solo on *Home, Sweet Home*, a serious song that enabled Cat to really communicate with the audience. Hovie agreed.

Cat had a habit of getting his body all out of shape when he was singing. He would bend over with his rear end sticking out in the funniest shape you ever saw, and would walk around on stage while singing.

When Cat struck up *Home, Sweet Home*, I came in the door at the rear of the audience, bent over in a stupid-looking position with my rear sticking out. I walked all the way down the center aisle, shaking hands with the people. The ripple of laughter that came up from the back of the house when I came in grew as I came on down the aisle and by the time I got to the stage, the crowd was broken up. They knew who I was mimicking.

Cat was almost crying. When I reached the front, he didn't even know what he was singing.

* * *

On and on it went, each of us trying to lick the other.

In Oklahoma City one night Cat really got to me. We had a big crowd and when the Blackwood Brothers got through our first song, someone in the back of the house yelled, "Cut down the bass mike." Thinking it was too loud, we cut it down a bit.

As we finished our second song, this guy hollered, "The bass mike's still too loud." So we took some more off it. After our third song, he yelled, "The bass is drowning everybody else," and we reduced the volume again.

At the end of the fourth song, he yelled, "I can still hear the bass," and I recognized the fool. It was Cat Freeman again. I jumped off the stage and chased him out of the auditorium.

*   *   *

Cat wasn't my only Jonah. Jake Hess was another. During the years of the Blackwood-Statesmen team, I could never get anything done as long as Jake was around. And when we were on stage, I had to be on my toes as long as Jake was in the building. He'd do anything to foul me up on stage.

We used to do fifteen or twenty Christmas shows every year at all these mills in Alabama and Georgia. Those mill people were some of our greatest fans, and we always had a good time entertaining them at Christmas.

Sometimes, if the quartet's singing wasn't stirring up the people, James would put me out there to do some comedy, and I always ended up by singing a solo. We were working a mill show in a high school auditorium in Alabama and James put me on for a comedy routine.

Jake, nosing around backstage, found the door of the band room unlocked and went in to inspect the instruments. He found the biggest bass drum in there that he'd ever seen. That thing looked to be five feet in diameter. He had to get help to get it strapped on, and someone handed him two of those big, padded drumsticks.

He waited till I was approaching the end of my song and came marching out on stage beating that drum in cadence with his marching, and I know you could hear the drum all over town. It just destroyed me. Those drumbeats began to echo in my ears and I even forgot what song I was singing.

The crowd was laughing so hard at Jake they didn't even realize I was still on stage.

When we came off and the Statesmen went on, I said to Hovie, "Put Jake on for a solo. He's made a fool out of me for the last time!" I went back to that band room and got a huge tuba, draped it over my shoulders and came out to wait in the wings for Jake to go on solo. I didn't let him see me with the tuba.

When Jake did his solo, I waited till he was on the last chorus and marched out on stage and stood beside him with that tuba draped over me, and Jake looked around and flinched. He knew what was coming. I had never blown a tuba in my life, and I waited till Jake came down to the final note in his solo, and I drew in my breath, put my mouth on that mouthpiece, and blew as hard as I could, with the tuba pointed right at a microphone.

Well, wouldn't you know that what came out of that tuba was the most perfect note anyone ever blew. It blended right in with Jake's final note, and the crowd thought it was a part of the show. The ending of that song really sounded great, and that crowd gave Jake a standing ovation! Those people almost tore up the place clapping for Jake, and I stood there with egg on my face thinking, "At least Jake didn't make a fool out of me this time—I did it to myself!"

* * *

I may have saved Wally Fowler's life one night in Nashville in an incident that turned out, some say, to be one of the funniest things I ever did on stage—and none of it was planned.

Two of Wally's big All-Night Sings were in Nashville's Ryman Auditorium on Friday night and in Atlanta's Municipal Auditorium the next night. On the Nashville sing, the last hour was always broadcast over WSM, which wouldn't give Wally permission to advertise the Atlanta sing the next evening unless he bought time on the program.

Wally was never one to let an obstacle stand in his path for very long. He began closing the Nashville show—on the air— with a prayer.

"Now, Lord," he would pray, "go with the Blackwood Brothers and Statesmen as they travel tonight the two hundred and fifty miles from here to Atlanta, Georgia, where they will appear tomorrow night at 7:30 in the Municipal Auditorium for another big Wally Fowler All-Night Sing, and where the people can buy their tickets in advance at Newberry's for two dollars a head. . . ." He'd even tell the Lord what Newberry's street address was—I suppose so the Lord would know exactly where to buy his tickets—and then he'd ask the Lord to bless all that. His prayer never reached heaven, I am sure, but it reached everybody listening to WSM. The director of the radio show thought it was so funny that he always kept the show on the air till Wally finished praying.

One night as Wally began his prayer, wringing wet with sweat because there wasn't any air-conditioning in the building then, to make sure that the radio mike picked him up, he reached over and got hold of it and drew it closer to him, and then grabbed the P.A. mike to pull it closer. Holding both of those mikes at the same time, Wally became a connector and all this electricity began flooding through his body.

I was standing in the wings where I could watch him and hear his prayer, and suddenly I saw him shaking and slowly sinking to his knees, and I realized he was being electrocuted.

Very quickly, I ran over and kicked the cord of the P.A. set out of the wall to shut off the current. Freed from the electricity, Wally sank to the floor, then made a miraculous recovery in front of that houseful of people. He came back to his feet, grabbed the P.A. mike, which someone quickly plugged back in, and, never one to miss an opportunity, said to the people, "Ladies and gentlemen, you have just witnessed a miracle of God. Here I stood, slowly being electrocuted to death, and God in his infinite mercy looked down on me and shut off the electricity that was killing me. . . ."

That's when I ran out on stage and shouted, "Wally, *I'm* the one that unplugged you!" And that crowd came apart at the seams, howling with laughter.

CHAPTER SIXTEEN

Elvis

Elvis Presley was one of my favorite people. When he was young he tried to become affiliated, in a round-about way, with the Blackwood Brothers.

Elvis grew up in Memphis and when I joined the Blackwood Brothers and moved to Memphis, Elvis was living in a low-rent housing project and driving a truck for a living. James and I used to let him into our concerts free at Ellis Auditorium because he couldn't afford to buy a ticket.

Elvis tried out with a quartet that Cecil Blackwood and Jim Hamill had, the Songfellows, and they turned him down. Said he wasn't good enough. This was one of Elvis's big jokes. Every time he saw one of us after he became successful, he'd laugh and ask, "How's the old boy who wouldn't give me a job with the Blackwood Brothers?" He didn't say "Song-fellows," he'd say "Blackwood Brothers," and when you come right down to it, I guess he could have sung with the Blackwood Brothers.

Soon after I came to Memphis, Elvis began getting hot as a singer. Early one morning we were going from Houston to Shreveport, Louisiana, clunking along in that first bus. I was driving and the other guys were asleep.

Suddenly this brand new El Dorado Cadillac came around us. I couldn't see who was driving, but I saw this good-looking girl sitting in the front seat, so I threw her a kiss, just cutting up.

The car slowed and I passed it, and here it came again, passing us. This time the girl waved and threw me a kiss.

We went on like this for a few miles, playing cat and mouse and laughing, breaking the monotony of the road.

Then we came to a small town and passing slowly through it, this Cadillac came around us and cut me off, forcing me into the curb. I thought, "Oh, oh, J. D., you've done it now."

But I couldn't run and when the fellow from the El Dorado came to the door of the bus, I opened it.

"Hi, Mr. Sumner," he said, "I'm Elvis Presley."

"Hello," I said, hugely relieved.

"Where are James and Cecil and the rest of the boys?" he asked. Then he saw them stirring in their reclining chairs and said, "Don't wake them. I was just passing by," and he grinned.

But I woke up the boys and we sat and talked with Elvis for a half hour. He, too, was returning from Houston where someone had given him the El Dorado.

In later years, I went to Elvis's house to visit with him—this was before he hired the Stamps Quartet to back him on stage—and found every record album made by the Blackwood Brothers, the Statesmen, the Imperials, the Stamps, and several other groups.

Elvis took the song *Without Him* off a Stamps Quartet album to record on his own RCA Victor record. This delighted us.

Elvis had an intercom in his house in Memphis. He kept a guard on the gate, and anytime he was home and any of us in gospel singing wanted to see him, all we had to do was identify ourselves to the guard and he ushered us right in.

Elvis thought a lot of gospel singing people, and we thought a lot of him. He used the Imperials, who were under contract to my talent agency, Sumar, to back him on records and on stage.

They were working Las Vegas once and I flew out to see their show and check on how the Imperials were doing. Elvis sent word to me to come down to his dressing room. He met me at the door and we shook hands. We talked for some time about what we were doing in gospel music, and about Jake Hess and James Blackwood and Hovie Lister and several others of his close friends.

If Elvis had done what he really wanted to do, I believe he

would be singing gospel music today. He used to come to our conventions and sing until his management made him stop.

When Elvis's mother died, they were members of the same church most of the Blackwood Brothers attended. We were on the road and Elvis called us in South Carolina and asked if we would sing at her funeral.

Of course, we said yes, and Elvis chartered a plane and flew us from Anderson, South Carolina, to Memphis for the funeral. We were supposed to sing four songs but Elvis kept sending up requests and we kept singing until we had sung twelve songs. Then he flew us back to Anderson for our performance that night.

* * *

The Stamps Quartet made a western swing early in 1970 and Elvis and the Imperials were playing the International Hotel in Las Vegas, so we stopped off on our way out to see a show.

I played golf in the afternoon, then told the boys to go see the first show that evening and we would leave for California just after the show.

Tony Brown, our pint-sized piano player, got mad about that. He wanted to see Elvis's last show; he'd heard it was better than the first. I had also promised Tony I would get Elvis to autograph a picture for Tony's wife who was a great Elvis fan.

When Tony got mad about having to miss the last show, he remarked, "All right, but don't forget my autographed picture—you can get it so easy."

So then I got mad. The thought of not getting the picture at all crossed my mind, but that wouldn't have been fair to Tony's wife, so after the first show I took Tony down to Elvis's dressing room.

There were several people out there sending their names in to Elvis, hoping to get in to see him. I told the policeman on guard outside Elvis's door to tell him that J. D. Sumner wanted in.

The policeman went inside and in a moment one of Elvis's sidekicks came out and said, "If J. D. Sumner, the long-legged bass singer, is out here, Elvis says come on in."

Elvis was eating a steak, as he did between shows. We

began talking about old times and Elvis verified my story about the girl in the Cadillac and some others that I had told Tony.

Then Elvis turned to Tony, whose hair had grown down over his collar, and said, "You gospel singers, man, started this long hair. I lost three jobs trying to grow my hair like a gospel singer. I used to look at J. D.'s hair when I was a kid and I'd say, man, that's for me. And that orange suit J. D. used to wear. I said this has gotta be for me. Gospel music."

Tony couldn't get over what a nice person Elvis was. Elvis was one star whose prominence didn't go to his head. And he absolutely had the most perfect face I've ever seen on a human being. It's no wonder the boy became a star. He was the best-looking man I'd ever seen. Tony remarked about what a handsome guy he was.

And Elvis took his work seriously. He went into training six weeks before he ever started a show. I mean physical training, running, exercising.

He was a karate expert, too. When he first became nationally prominent, he had to whip four or five guys who thought if they could beat the daylights out of Elvis Presley they'd be king-pins.

Once in Memphis a fellow, whose wife was crazy about Elvis's singing, saw Elvis getting gasoline at a Texaco station and told him he was going to whip him. Elvis had never seen either the man or his wife before, but the guy came at him— and Elvis almost killed him.

There are a lot of kooks in the world, and in a business like Elvis's was, I guess you'd meet most of them.

We sat there talking for a while, and Elvis autographed a picture for Tony's wife, and Tony finally said, "I can't believe it."

"Can't believe what, son?" Elvis asked. I always called Tony "son" and Elvis adopted it unconsciously.

"You talk just like we do," Tony said.

CHAPTER SEVENTEEN

Low Notes

Low notes have never scared me. I was blessed with a voice low enough to handle any gospel song that's ever been written. But for any bass singer to have a good night, everything has to go just so. The sound has to be right, the quality of the sound has to be so that the singer can hear it. If you can't hear it, you can't hit it. You have to feel like singing, and your voice must be cooperating. It helps to be singing in a building with good acoustics. There are few professional singers whose voices aren't trained to do just what the mind orders, but there are many convention singers who'll tell you that there are days when they just can't sing a lick.

I never have completely failed to reach a note. I've failed the first time. I've had to try as high as five times, but I've never failed yet to reach the note I want.

Most bass singers get fouled up if they fail to reach their note the first time, but not me. I'll make a crack to the audience, like, "Well, you couldn't hit it either. If you think you can, come up here and we'll try it together." Then I'll take another stab at it.

My voice wasn't always as low as it is now. It went down considerably after I joined the Blackwood Brothers, because it hadn't matured before that. For a long time during those Blackwood years I found myself going deeper and deeper.

A funny thing about singing bass is how much altitude has to do with your voice. The whole time I sang with the Sunshine Boys in Wheeling I couldn't hit anything but a C and an occasional B flat, but when we moved back down to Atlanta, my voice dropped lower.

The higher the elevation the higher you sing, the lower the elevation the lower you sing. It's that simple.

In Denver, for example, the altitude is a mile high and it's hard for a flatlander to go to Denver and just breathe, let alone sing.

Well, it really isn't quite that tough. I can go out there with my quartet and sing about as low as I want to—but if I stayed there a while my voice would rise.

If I lived there a year I guess I'd be a tenor.

Confidence is another thing a bass singer needs. I got mine from a fellow named Si Langlois.

When I was with the Sunshine Boys, we used to go to New York and cut transcriptions. They were called Langworth Transcriptions and were played over about six hundred radio stations.

We'd sing several songs and they would put them on large records, three or four on each side. Back then there wasn't anything but 78 and 45 rpm records, but they would take a 45 and turn it into a 33 1/3.

The people who cut transcriptions and the radio stations that used them were advanced. They were using 33 1/3 a long time before anybody else, and their transcriptions were fantastic records of the highest quality.

We'd go to New York twice a year and record about three days at a time.

Si Langlois was in the control room when we cut these records and his voice was belly-deep; he could really get on down.

He always complimented me on how good my voice was. I guess he just liked bass singers since he was one himself.

But he did more than that for me. If I couldn't hit a note in a song we were transcribing, he'd hit it for me and you couldn't tell the difference. Then later he would show me how to hit it.

He also told me never to sing on anything but a ribbon mike, that my voice sounded much better on a ribbon mike than it did on any other kind.

Yes, Si Langlois was a fine man who did a lot for me.

*   *   *

A YOUNG AND LOVELY MARY

LEFT: *COURTSHIP DAY WITH MARY*

RIGHT: *THEY POSED FOR THIS PICTURE BEFORE J.D. WENT INTO THE SERVICE*

WEDDING DAY

ARMY DAYS

MUSIC IN THE EARLY DAYS/SUNNY SOUTH QUARTET
Jake Hess, Horace Floyd, J.D., Roger Clark and Quentin Hicks

WHEELING DAYS

MAY, 1951

FRONT ROW: Hiram Hayseed, Chickie Williams, Abbie Neal, Juanita Moore, Gay Franzi, Wilma Lee Cooper, Dusty Brown, Ann Jones, Krazy Elmer.

MIDDLE ROW: Wyn Sheldon, Lee Moore, Cy Williams, Doc Williams, Ace Richman, Red Smiley, J. D. Sumner, Roy Scott, Marion Martin, Pete Cassell, Jimmy Carson, Cowboy Phil, Lew Clawson.

BACK ROW: Jackie Phelps, Eddie Wallace, Toby Stroud, Bill Carver, Stoney Cooper, Monty Blake, Freddie Daniels, Gene Jenkins, Don Reno.

WWVA JAMBOREE/SUNSHINE BOYS

SUNSHINE BOYS

HOLLYWOOD AND THE MOVIES

BLACKWOOD DAYS

J.D. BUYS HOME FOR MOM AND DAD IN FLORIDA

TAKING CARE OF BUSINESS

ON STAGE

A FAVORITE PASTIME

J.D. NEVER USED HIS TRADE BUT HE IS A QUALIFIED WATCH REPAIR MAN

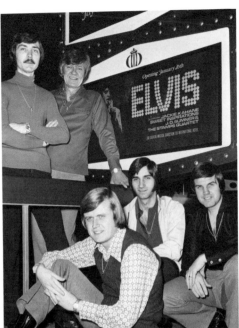

CARS HAVE ALWAYS BEEN A SPECIAL HOBBY FOR J.D.

SUNSHINE BOYS REUNION

THE MASTERS FIVE
WITH THE
GATLIN BROTHERS

SOUVENIR PROGRAM

GOSPEL MUSIC NEWS
presents the Third Annual
"ROAST"
honoring
J.D. SUMNER

Wednesday, October 2, 1985
Hyatt Regency
Ballrooms 2, 3 & 4

INVOCATION
Rev. Doug Westmoreland - Tusculum Hills Baptist Church
LUNCHEON
ROAST MASTER
Jerry Goff
ROASTERS:
HAROLD REID / The Statlers
DON REID / The Statlers
PHIL BALSLEY / The Statlers
JIMMY FORTUNE / The Statlers
GEORGE YOUNCE / The Cathedrals
TAMMY WYNETTE / The First Lady of Country Music
BECKY HUGHES / Gospel Music News
RICHARD STERBAN / The Oak Ridge Boys
HOVIE LISTER / The Masters V
CONNIE HOPPER / The Queen of Gospel Music
RAY STEVENS / Country Music Entertainer
JAMES BLACKWOOD / The Masters V
JAKE HESS / The Masters V
WENDY BAGWELL / Wendy Bagwell and the Sunliters
REBUTTAL
J.D. Sumner
HOSTED BY
Becky Hughes & Gospel Music News
COORDINATOR
Pat Mathis
Pre-roast music courtesy of C.J. Almgren

A FUN DAY FOR
J.D. AND FRIENDS,
1985 ROAST

TAMMY WYNETTE, J.D. AND RAY STEVENS AT 1985 ROAST

STATLER BROTHERS SING SONG THEY WROTE
ESPECIALLY FOR J.D.'S ROAST, 1985

RUDY AND LARRY GATLIN BACKSTAGE WITH J.D.

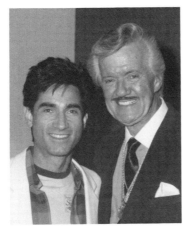

LEFT: *RICHARD STERBAN WITH MENTOR J.D.*
RIGHT: *J.D. POSES WITH PAL GERALDO*

SPECIAL FRIEND RONNIE MILSAP IN REHEARSAL
WITH J.D. FOR TNN APPEARANCE.

J.D. ON STAGE WITH TENNESSEE ERNIE FORD, CECIL AND JIMMY BLACKWOOD

THROUGH THE YEARS WITH PAL JAKE HESS

TNN SPECIAL BY INVITATION OF TAMMY WYNETTE (J.D., JAMES BLACKWOOD, TAMMY WYNETTE, JAKE HESS AND BILL GAITHER). THANK YOU, TAMMY—LOVE, J.D.

BILL BAIZE, ED ENOCH, DAVE ROWLAND AND J.D.

J.D. LOOKS ON WITH PRIDE! BILL BAIZE (Miss Mary's favorite tenor), DONNIE SUMNER, ED ENOCH, RICHARD STERBAN AND THE BOSS

JIM HILL, J.D., TONY BROWN, DONNIE SUMNER, MYLON LEFEVRE AND JIMMY BLACKWOOD

TONY BROWN, KEN HICKS, JIMMY (DUKE) DUMAS, BILL BAIZE, ED ENOCH, DONNIE SUMNER AND RICHARD STERBAN

JIM HILL, J.D., JIMMY BLACKWOOD, JIMMY DUMAS, TONY BROWN, DONNIE SUMNER AND MYLON LEFEVRE

TIM BEATY, BILLY BLACKWOOD, TONY BROWN, JIMMY DUMAS, JIM HILL, DONNIE SUMNER, J.D. AND JIMMY BLACKWOOD.

C.J. ALMGREN, J.D., RICK STRICKLAND, ED HILL AND ED ENOCH

"GRAND OLE OPRY APPEARANCE"
CURRENT STAMPS: RICK STRICKLAND, ED ENOCH, ED HILL, AND J.D.
KEYBOARD (C.J. ALMGREN NOT SHOWN)

STAMPS APPEARANCE ON MUSIC CITY TONIGHT WITH LORIANNE CROOK
AND CHARLIE CHASE.

THANK YOU, PRISCILLA AND LISA MARIE, JACK SNOWDEN, TODD MORGAN,
PATSY ANDERSON, GRACELAND AND ELVIS PRESLEY ENTERPRISES, INC.
WARMEST REGARDS ALWAYS, J.D. AND THE STAMPS

Graceland

"J.D.'S LOVE AND RELATIONSHIP WITH ELVIS CONTINUES"

MOM AND DAD—LEILA LEE SUMNER AND JOHN SUMNER

J.D. WITH SISTERS MYRTIS MATHEWS, BERNICE THOMPSON AND BROTHER
BUDDY SUMNER CELEBRATING BIRTHDAY FOR MOM, 1986

LEFT: A SPECIAL MOTHER'S DAY (MAMA, LEILA SUMNER, WAS PICKED
UP FOR CHURCH IN LIMO, ROSES WERE WAITING FOR HER ARRIVAL,
THEN TREATED TO LUNCH AND RETURN RIDE HOME. J.D. ENJOYED
SURPRISING HER.
RIGHT: JIM AND SALLY ENOCH WITH GRANDSON JASON AT STAMPS CONCERT

"HOLIDAYS"
FRANCES, SHIRLEY AND JASON ASSISTING NANA IN KITCHEN

CHRISTMAS MEMORIES

LEFT: *MARY WITH HER BROTHERS AND SISTER, DECEMBER, 1985*
RIGHT: *MARY SUMNER, MIM BLACKWOOD AND SHIRLEY ENOCH*

FAMILY FAVORITES OF NANA AND BIGDADDY

LEFT: *MISS MARY IN EUROPE WITH J.D. AND THE STAMPS*

LEFT: *A HAPPY DAY AT THE BEACH IN GULF SHORES ON TOUR WITH J.D.*
"A FAMILY FAVORITE OF MISS MARY"
RIGHT: *MARY AND THE SMILE SHE HAD FOR EVERYONE*

LEFT: *FRANCES, 1943*
RIGHT: *OLDER SISTER FRANCES HOLDING BABY SISTER SHIRLEY*

LEFT: *FRANCES SUMNER DUNN WITH BROTHERS PETE ON LEFT AND DONNIE SUMNER ON RIGHT*
RIGHT: *FRANCES WITH HUSBAND JIM DUNN*

LEFT: *"A PROUD GREAT-GRANDMOTHER" IF YOU CAN BELIEVE THAT! DAUGHTER FRANCES AND GREAT-GRANDDAUGHTER JORDAN*
RIGHT: *KATHY JONES HALL/GRANDDAUGHTER*

LEFT: *KATHY, NANA AND BIGDADDY'S ADORABLE LITTLE LADY*
RIGHT: *KATHY ALL GROWN UP AND READY TO GRADUATE*

LEFT: *KATHY AND HUSBAND GREG HALL*
RIGHT: *JORDAN HALL/GREAT-GRANDDAUGHTER*

LEFT: *DENVER HALL/GREAT-GRANDSON*
RIGHT: *SHIRLEY AND HER FAVORITE BABY DOLL*

LEFT: *SHIRLEY ENJOYING AN ELVIS SHOW WITH THE STAMPS IN VEGAS*
RIGHT: *SHIRLEY WITH JASON'S DAD AND LONG STAMPS LEAD ED ENOCH*

LEFT: *SHIRLEY PREPARING DRESSING BY MOM'S RECIPE DURING CHRISTMAS*
RIGHT: *SHIRLEY AND SON JASON ENOCH, 1991 ANNIVERSARY PARTY FOR NANA AND BIGDADDY*

LEFT: *JASON DANIEL ENOCH*
RIGHT: *BIGDADDY WITH HIS MAIN MAN/GRANDSON JASON*

LEFT: *MOM, THIS IS JUST FOR YOU—JASON, "I HATE DOING THIS"*
RIGHT: *BIGDADDY USED TO BE A COWBOY? (JASON)*

LEFT: *JASON DANIEL ENOCH*
RIGHT: *LOVED THAT NANA, BUT WHO DIDN'T*

LEFT: *50TH WEDDING ANNIVERSARY*
RIGHT: *MISS MARY TO MR. J.D.*

LEFT: *GREAT-GRANDDAUGHTER JORDAN WITH MOM KATHY
AT 50TH CELEBRATION*
RIGHT: *JASON AND PROUD DAD ED AT ANNIVERSARY PARTY*

JASON AND KATHY WITH NANA AND BIGDADDY AS THEY ARRIVE AT SURPRISE ANNIVERSARY PARTY

JASON, NANA AND BIGDADDY

THANK YOU,
MARY AND J.D. SUMNER

MR. AND MRS. J.D. SUMNER, JUNE 14, 1991, CELEBRATE THEIR 50TH WEDDING ANNIVERSARY

A bass singer is entirely dependent on his sound system. In fact, the entire quartet leans heavily on its sound system to satisfy an audience. The P. A. enables you to sing as loud or as low as necessary to project a mood.

Sound systems give quartets balance, and sound either makes or breaks a quartet. We could no more put on a satisfying performance today without a good sound system than we could fly, but we still have people come up and say they'd love to hear us sing without the P. A. They don't realize that in our business amplification is everything.

Neither London Parris nor I—and we were recognized as the two lowest basses in the business—could ever produce F below low C without a sound system.

We sing arrangements two steps below the key they're written in, and we can do this only because we have proper amplification. We sing songs in such a low key that even the baritone couldn't be heard across the stage if it weren't for the sound system.

Unfortunately, not every quartet knows how to use this tool. But it is part of the training that people in most major professional groups undergo. We operate our own sound. We run the bass mike pretty high and any time a guy has a lead by himself, we build up the volume on his mike.

The Stamps Quartet, which I took over in 1965, was the first to go to four mikes. Remember, when I went with the Blackwood Brothers, James let me build a new sound system and for the first time we used two microphones for the quartet. When I took over the Stamps Quartet, we extended this thinking and gave each singer his own mike. This makes it easier to balance the sound. It's the same principle used in recording studios where they use eight tracks, one for each singer and four others for various instruments. Regardless of who sings loudest or plays loudest during the session, they can balance the blend in the recording.

Basically we tried to operate our sound on stage the same way. We had eight channels in our sound system in those days—the late sixties—two pre-amps and one master amp. We ran the piano off one mike, the rhythm guitar off another, the bass guitar off still another, and there was one the drums could use, when we had drums, but we didn't use it for them: They were usually loud enough without amplification. Then we had four mikes for the quartet, and another (the one the drummer didn't use) that the piano player could sing through when we wanted him to.

I operated the sound system myself. If the control panel had to be placed offstage, I gave signals to whoever operated it. If we wanted more piano, I made a motion like I'm playing a piano and he'd raise the volume. Then we used a one, two, three, four signal for the singers. If I held up one finger, it meant adjust the bass up or down, depending on whether I pointed the finger up or down. Two fingers meant the baritone, three the lead, and four the tenor.

Sound is so important to our programs that we carry our own systems. Most of the top gospel singing groups own their own equipment and put thousands of dollars into buying it. We have better sound systems than most auditoriums, who spend many thousands of dollars for a set-up that isn't adequate for quartets.

*   *   *

For many years I have been billed as the lowest bass singer in the world, a billing once enjoyed by my old friend Arnold Hyles of the Rangers Quartet.

We didn't dream up the billing for me either in a sense of boasting or to be funny. There simply wasn't a bass singer who had sung as low as I. At least no one had it on record if they had.

I have a double low C recorded on one of our albums and many Gs, Fs, and E flats. I also hit a double low C on an album with Elvis when the Stamps Quartet backed him, and I was carried six years in the *Guinness Book of World Records* for having recorded the lowest note ever. This is no big deal, I suppose, because when a bass goes below an F it's hard to tell how deep he really is anyway. Down there, one note sounds about the same as another to an untrained ear. Sometimes, only the singer himself can tell.

To sing that low constantly, a bass singer must have more going for him than the depth of his voice and the proper sound equipment.

He must have confidence that he can get down there whenever he wants to, or needs to.

There is a little man in the back of your head who keeps

telling you that you can't do thus and so, that other people can do this better than you, and that you're in danger of losing this and losing that.

He's a darned pest, but he's real. And before a bass singer can reach his goals—or can consistently reach those low notes—he's got to subdue this little man.

I was struck by the little fellow soon after the Blackwood Brothers began riding that first old bus, and I licked him quickly.

We were heading for Augusta, Georgia, to sing on a program with the Rebels Quartet. London Parris, who hadn't been in the business too long, was singing bass for the Rebels, and London was really low. Fact is, London was the only challenge to those low notes that I had then.

For some reason, there at first, when I was around him he bugged me. He felt the same about me. He was a threat to my dominance of those double low Cs.

We were on the road to Augusta that afternoon when Jackie Marshall, who always had a penchant for getting my goat, suddenly said, "J. D., London's going to put it on you tonight."

I laughed and tried to put off the feeling that he was right, but that little man chimed in, "Jackie's right, you know; he's telling the truth. London Parris *is* going to put it on you tonight."

I tried to ignore that little man—but I couldn't ignore Jackie. No one could do that. Jackie must have seen that his barb had gone deep, for he really began twisting it, jabbing, needling, making me sore, with that little man helping him all the way.

Finally, I got mad. I got out of my reclining chair and went to the front of the bus and jabbed a finger at Jackie. "Little man, I want to tell you one thing," I said. "Tonight in Augusta, if I don't sing two steps lower than London Parris, I'll quit. I'll quit tonight. I'll just walk off the stage and never come back."

James saw that I'd backed myself into a corner, with a little push from Jackie, and he knew I was serious.

"Now wait a minute," James said. "Jackie's just been cutting up. You shut up, Jackie, and let's forget this. It doesn't make any difference who sings the lowest. It makes no difference at all."

I looked around and the only way out of that corner was straight over Jackie.

"No," I said, "we're not going to forget nothing. And it does make a difference, James. Tonight you make sure they go on before we do and I'm going to tell London to sing as low as he can, then if I don't sing the same song two steps lower, you'll have to find another bass singer."

I stalked back to my chair and sat down. James continued to try to talk me out of it, but I told him I meant what I said. "I'll quit, James; you know I will." He knew it, too.

By the time we got to Augusta I was really mad. I suppose subconsciously I was also trying to lick that little man, but I was only thinking of what I had to do.

I looked up London, who was one of the finest and friendliest guys in the business, and told him to sing *I Can Tell You Now the Time*, and to drop it as low as he could.

I don't know whether anyone else talked to him or whether he sang as low as he could, but we were all listening in the wings and he put it way on down there in the low, low range.

We were perhaps the grimmest quartet that ever went before the mikes that night. I was determined to beat that little man, and the other fellows, including Jackie Marshall by this time, were hoping I could. But I didn't know whether I could or not.

We sang a couple of songs, then struck up *I Can Tell You Now the Time*, and sure enough, we dropped it down two steps lower than the Rebels and I didn't miss a note.

The sweat was rolling off all the guys as we went lower and lower, and when I finally hit the note I wanted, you could feel the tension lift like a great weight.

And that little man headed for the boondocks.

From that day to this, I have never been worried by another bass singer—nor by that little man. It isn't that I think I'm better than any other bass, but when I whipped the little man, I was freed from my shackles. I think I have been a better bass singer since that night.

But if I hadn't hit that note, I know that I'd have quit singing that night.

*   *   *

I have a double low C recorded with the Stamps Quartet on *Blessed Assurance*. The night the baby cried, I went down to a low F below low C.

I've always followed this rule about singing low: When I go down to get a low note, I go just a hair below it and come back up to it. Most singers don't do it that way, but I'm fortunate that my voice is low enough to allow me that leeway.

If I have to hit an F, instead of going directly to it I go just a fraction below it, then come back to the F.

I do it that way for a reason. If you don't get all the way down to the note you want and you happen to be sharp when you stop, you can't go on until you hit the proper note. You've already got your vocal cords set, and your breathing is set, and that's where you'll stop. So when I go down to F, I go to about an E or E flat and come back up to the F.

The day we recorded *Blessed Assurance* and I hit the double low C, my voice broke a speaker.

After a song is put on tape during a recording session, they play it back pretty loud to listen for flaws. When they played this one back and I hit the double low C, one of the speakers burst in a big A-7 Voice of the Theater set we were using.

The bass voice vibrates the same as the tenor voice. You've heard stories of how Enrico Caruso broke glasses across the room with his tenor voice, because of the shrill and fast vibrations. The bass voice can do the same thing.

People have told me that their stereo sets have actually walked on the floor when I hit a real low note on a record. I couldn't vouch for this, though; my stereo never did.

* * *

It's strange that when most people asked if I could sing lower than this fellow or that one, the name most often mentioned was not London Parris but Larry Hooper, the bass singer on the Lawrence Welk Show for many years.

London and I had sung on so many programs together that most people who came to hear us had made up their minds that I was lower than London or vice versa.

But there were few yardsticks for measuring my voice against Larry Hooper's. I guess London was in the same boat; he probably got the same questions I did.

Once the Stamps Quartet was booked to work a fair in

Goodland, Kansas, and Larry was to be on the same program.

Larry wasn't singing on the matinee, just on the night show. The Stamps Quartet was booked to sing both.

In the afternoon, I kept thinking about what all those people had asked me, and I began to wonder, too, whether I was lower than Larry.

Now these doubts weren't raised by that little man I had laid away several years earlier, but by another little fellow with a pitchfork tail and two horns growing out of his head.

Deep down I knew it didn't really matter whether I could sing as low as Larry Hooper, but by the time that little guy with the horns got through with me, I had made up my mind to find out.

At the matinee, I put on a show. I sang every low song that I could think of, and apparently did a pretty good job, because when we left the stage the fair manager sent for me.

"Now, look," the manager said. "You're a lower singer than Larry Hooper, but you're not here to make a fool of him."

"The last thing in my mind is to make a fool of Mr. Hooper," I said honestly. "I just wanted to satisfy myself that I can sing the lowest."

After all, I had that lowest-bass-singer-in-the-world reputation to live up to.

"I don't care what you have to satisfy," he said. "Tonight let's have some singing with all four harmony parts. I don't want any of that low singing."

That's like asking a batter not to swing at the ball.

He even named some of the songs I wouldn't be allowed to sing that night, and one was *Just a Closer Walk with Thee* in which all I hit is a B flat.

"I'm gonna be standing back there listening," he said, "and if you try any funny stuff, so help me, I'll pull the plug on you."

When we went on stage that night, I didn't obey the fair manager entirely. We sang mostly harmony stuff, but I did throw in a pretty low note here and there. Those people hadn't come to hear me sing tenor.

I'm not telling this story to embarrass Mr. Hooper. He was really lower than I had anticipated; he is a terrific singer, and a fine gentleman to boot. After I satisfied my ego in the afternoon, I thoroughly enjoyed being on the same show with him.

And Tony Brown and Duke Dumas and the other guys in our quartet who really know music—I'm not one of them— said that Larry is a fantastic piano player.

*   *   *

Whether I could sing as low after the operation on my throat was a question I got from many audiences. There was a reason folks didn't notice the depth of my voice as much as they once did.

The answer to the question is yes, I sang just as low after the operation. I've been that low ever since, maybe lower, and that's been a quarter of a century. A bass singer's voice usually begins to deteriorate about the age of fifty-five, but mine didn't. I always had perfect pitch—that's what other musicians and voice teachers told me—and I can still hit the notes in the middle. When I can no longer do that, I'll quit.

The reason folks didn't notice how low I could sing as much as they once had was because I was no longer a sideman. When I took over the Stamps Quartet, the show became mine to run, and I had a responsibility toward the other six men of the quartet who performed on stage.

When the Blackwood Brothers went into a town where people really loved bass singing, James would wear me out. But in the Stamps Quartet we had so much excellent young talent that I felt I had to give each of them enough time to show the people what they could do. By the time I'd get those cats on for one song each, there wasn't much time left for the low stuff.

But I was happy. I no longer had to prove to anyone how low I could sing. It was all on the record. It still is.

I got a bigger kick out of exhibiting the kids of the Stamps Quartet than I did shaking a building with double low Cs.

*   *   *

Big Chief and London, both of whom are now gone, and bass singers of that type will never be replaced. They were of the type that George Younce and I came from.

London died only a while before the rewriting of this book, so let me say something about him, and I mean this from the heart: If London Parris had had my mental attitude, he would have been the best bass singer who ever lived. London's problem was that he never believed in himself the way J. D. Sumner believes. I licked that little man inside me who tried to keep me from singing my best, but London never did whip the little man inside himself.

London Parris inspired me. When he would come out and sit in the audience to hear me sing, I would say, "Okay, London, you are fixing to hear how bass is supposed to be sung." On the other hand, when I went out and sat to hear him sing, it would tear him all to pieces.

Big Chief was a rhythm bass, perfect for the Statesmen. He was the best rhythm bass in the business, and, I suspect, the best there will ever be.

I want to say something about Rex Nelon, too. He was a tremendous bass until he tried to go almost contemporary. That, of course, was because he had his daughter, Kelly Nelon Thompson, and another girl singing with him and he wanted to sing what they sang best. But I remember the days when Rex Nelon was a great bass singer. I have begged him and begged him to get a male quartet and start singing bass again. He was a star, man, but today the way they sing, he's almost in the way. He was cut out for a male quartet, and that's where he ought to be singing.

CHAPTER EIGHTEEN

The Stamps Quartet

It was almost by accident that I left the Blackwood Brothers Quartet. We sang together eleven years, from 1954 to 1965, and there probably has never been a better-natured quartet on the road. We had a few minor difficulties like anyone will have who live and work together, but we got along amazingly well.

In those eleven years we had no personnel changes among the singers. Our only changes were at the piano. When Jackie Marshall left to go into private business, James hired Wally Varner, and Wally's style of play, like Jackie's, was perfect for the Blackwood Brothers.

The way Wally tinkled a piano not only blended well with singing voices but thrilled the crowds no end. Our only problem with Wally was his looks. He was short and stocky, had beady eyes and curly black hair, and wore a thin mustache.

We bought a set of dark blue, double-breasted, pin-striped suits and when Wally put his on he looked like he'd just come back from the St. Valentine's Day massacre. He looked like a gangster.

But he could play that piano.

After Wally left the Blackwood Brothers to settle down in private business, we changed the piano player another time or two, and those were the only changes for the quartet until I switched over to the Stamps Quartet. James and Cecil and Bill Shaw stayed with the quartet for several more years. They eventually got London Parris to sing bass, and what a whale of a job he did. Their harmony was so high they had to have a deep bass to balance the blend.

In 1963 we were casting around for a music company we could buy. We had looked into the James D. Vaughan Music Company but hadn't decided anything. One night in Will Rogers Auditorium in Fort Worth, Frank Stamps walked into the dressing room and came up to me.

"I hear you're interested in buying a music company," he said.

"Well, sir," I said, "I've been looking at one."

He said, "If you're going to buy one, why don't you buy a good one? I would like to sell mine. I've got a little money put back and I want to retire and do a little fishing."

Of course, I was interested, but I didn't know what to say at the moment. He continued:

"I'm very proud of the work my music company has done, and I want to see it continued. I have been watching you down through the years and feel you would be most capable of carrying on the work I have done."

So we negotiated, and James and Cecil and I bought the Stamps Quartet Music Company.

In the deal, we also inherited the Stamps Quartet. At that time it was not a professional quartet. It sang at singing conventions and things like that and while it was good, it was not the type of quartet that could compete with professional people on the road.

There are great differences in convention quartets and professional quartets.

Gradually we improved the Stamps Quartet until in 1964 we decided to make it a professional quartet and put it on the road. We hired Joe Roper from the Prophets Quartet and made him manager of the Stamps. Joe was a good pianist. He was the first piano player the Blackwood Brothers ever had, back in the thirties—so he became the Stamps' pianist in addition to managing the quartet.

We got Jerry Redd to sing tenor, Roger McDuff for the lead, Terry Blackwood for the baritone, and Big John Hall for the bass.

As the next order of business, we moved the quartet's headquarters from Fort Worth to Memphis.

The quartet didn't catch on like we hoped it would, so we hired Jim Hill from the Golden Keys Quartet in Portsmouth,

Ohio, and put him in as manager and tenor singer in Jerry Redd's place.

We needed an editor in the plant where we published song books and did some other printing, so we moved Joe Roper into that position and signed Chuck Ramsey to play for the quartet.

Still, things didn't work out. We were losing money too fast. Sometime before that, James Blackwood had allowed his son, James, Jr., and Winston Blackwood, Ronnie Blackwood, Bill Lyles, Jr., and Everett Reeves to form the Junior Blackwood Brothers, and their venture was about forty thousand dollars in the hole. The Stamps Quartet was also down about forty thousand, and when you're eighty thousand in the red you've got to back off and take another look. You've got something to worry about.

I felt the only way we could pull out would be for me to go with the Stamps Quartet to manage it and see that things were done the best they could be done.

James didn't take to that idea too well, and I didn't really want to leave what I considered to be the number one quartet in the business and move down to a group that would have rated thirty-fifth at best. But there was no other way that I could see.

So in 1965 I moved to the Stamps Quartet and Big John Hall switched from the Stamps to sing bass for the Blackwood Brothers.

When I made this move, I retained my interest in the Blackwood Brothers Quartet.

Before I joined the Blackwood Brothers, it was owned by Roy, Doyle, James, and R. W. Blackwood. The first three are brothers, and R. W. was Roy's son.

After the airplane crash, they dissolved that partnership and decided that the quartet members should own the quartet. Roy and Doyle continued to operate other ventures the Blackwood Brothers were in.

When Cecil and I joined the Blackwood Brothers in 1954, Cecil came on salary and I took an equal partnership. There were four partners: James, Jackie Marshall, Bill Shaw, and me. Cecil remained on salary for six or eight months, then he, too, became a partner, making five shares.

We have always had a buy-and-sell agreement that stipulates a member leaving a group has to sell his share to whoever takes his place, so when Jackie left, he sold his share to Wally Varner. The price ran around $3,500 and included Jackie's share of records, equipment like the bus and sound system, and things like that.

When Wally left, the four remaining members bought him out and decided that we would retain ownership of the quartet and take in any future members on salary. We did this because our operations were becoming so complex that the quartet's activities were only a part of the whole. So we hired Whitey Gleason on salary to replace Wally at the piano.

We did not exercise the buy-and-sell agreement when I left the Blackwood Brothers because I was tied up in all the other things in which the Blackwood Brothers were involved—and these were many.

So our arrangement became this: James, Cecil, Bill Shaw, and I owned the Blackwood Brothers Quartet, and James, Cecil, and I owned the Stamps Quartet. It really wasn't as confusing as it sounded; it was an arrangement that worked quite well for us.

Our agreement was simple: It was my responsibility to run the Stamps Quartet and James's responsibility to operate the Blackwood Brothers Quartet. We didn't interfere with each other, and it was a very good working arrangement.

I managed all our music companies: the Gospel Quartet Music Company, the Stamps Quartet Music Company, and the Temple Music Company.

*   *   *

When I switched to the Stamps Quartet, I thought it ironic that I got off a fine, air-conditioned bus, one of the best in the business, and crawled aboard another clunker like we'd started with ten years before. The Stamps bus was not air-conditioned, it was hot, and it was no mechanical marvel. But with the proper coaxing and kicking, it got us where we wanted to go.

There were a couple more quick personnel changes when I joined the Stamps. Terry Blackwood left the group to continue his education, and Mylon LeFevre replaced him. Then Mylon also left, and we put James Blackwood, Jr., to singing baritone.

So we had Jim Hill, Roger McDuff, Jimmy Blackwood, and me on the singing parts, and Chuck Ramsey playing piano.

Business picked up, but not to the point that I wanted to reach. We didn't have the sound I wanted, a new sound that would appeal to young and old alike.

The next member to leave was Ramsey, and I immediately brought my nephew, Donnie Sumner, Buddy's son, into the quartet to play the piano. Donnie is a talented young man, who can do about anything he wants in the field of music. He had been working in our publishing plant in Dallas before we put him on the stage.

For some time Roger McDuff had been wanting to go with his brothers, the McDuff Brothers. When I became involved with the management of the Stamps Quartet, I went all the way, picking out the programs we used on stage and things like that, which may not have set too well with Roger, who resigned.

Roger was a magnificent master of ceremonies, a job that I took over when he left, and I soon discovered that adding that job to my other tasks gave me a tighter control over the quartet and enabled me to do many things, particularly on stage, that I wanted to do but hadn't been able to before.

When Roger left in early 1966, I moved Donnie to lead singer and hired Tony Brown—we called him Tarzan—as pianist. Tarzan had attended our Stamps Quartet School of Music in Texas for four years and was an accomplished pianist. I didn't know him too well, but Don Butler knew him from the school.

Don had been business administrator for the Stamps-Blackwood Enterprises and was then headquartered in Atlanta as executive producer of the Statesmen-Blackwood jointly-owned *Singin' Time in Dixie* and *Glory Road* television programs. I asked Don to contact Tony and offer him the job of playing piano for the Stamps Quartet. Tarzan was with the Klaudt Indian Family and when Don called him and offered him the job, Tony asked if Don could hold the phone a minute. Returning to the phone a few seconds later, Tony accepted the job, no questions asked.

Later, Tony asked Don if he knew why he had asked him to hold the phone. Tony said he put the phone down and ran out in the front yard of his parents' home and screamed for joy at the top of his lungs. I suppose you could say from that that Tony was excited and happy about joining the Stamps Quartet.

Tony flew to Boston and joined us there on the first of February, 1966. He was eighteen, looked about twelve, and was an immediate hit. The young people in the audience went for his nutty antics on stage, and it wasn't long after he joined us that he became my straight man, or I became his—I don't know which. But I do know that he got a lot of laughs.

Our sound improved by the day and we began to pull the Stamps Quartet out of the woods. We had tremendous harmony, and wherever we sang people asked us back. They enjoyed the Stamps Quartet.

Shortly after we hired Tarzan, Mylon LeFevre came to me and said he wanted to come back with the Stamps Quartet. He said he didn't care whether I hired him or not, that he was going to get on the bus and go with us.

"If you can pay me, fine," Mylon said. "If you can't pay me, that's all right, too. But I'm going."

We took him on as bass guitar player. And we paid him.

*   *   *

In the summer of 1966 we moved from Memphis to Nashville. In June we were conducting the Stamps School of Music in Waxahachie, Texas, and I went to Jake Hess, who had left the Statesmen to organize the Imperials, and suggested that the Stamps move to Nashville and form a team with the Imperials. Jake had Sherrill Neilson on tenor, himself on lead, Gary McSpadden on baritone, and Armond Morales singing bass. Henry Slaughter was his piano player.

The move made better sense to me the more I thought about it. I felt as long as we were based in Memphis with the Blackwood Brothers that we would be considered as riding their coat tails, and I could see that the Stamps Quartet was going to be able to stand on its own feet.

We settled down in Nashville and Mylon persuaded us—it didn't take much persuasion—to look for a guitar player. I had heard of one in Crossett, Arkansas. Brock and Ben Speer told me of a boy down there who was really good. His name was Jimmy Dumas, but people called him Duke.

I called Dumas, who was working in a paper mill in Crossett, and asked him to meet us in Little Rock where we had a concert scheduled early in 1967. He said he would be there.

When Duke walked into the Marion Hotel in Little Rock, where we were staying, he looked more like a country boy than anyone I've ever seen. He had a crew cut, was dressed in jeans, and had a real country twang in his voice.

But he could evermore play that guitar!

He played for us at the hotel that afternoon in a tryout session and didn't miss a chord in any of our arrangements, and they were all new to him. He seemed to have a great ear for music, and certainly he had as much music in his fingertips as any guitarist I've ever seen.

We took him on stage at the concert that night to see how the crowd would affect him. Again he was perfect, didn't miss a note. He was fantastic, the crowd loved him, and he wasn't at all fearful of playing before an audience.

I hired him on the spot, feeling he would add a lot of excitement to our group.

Now to backpedal a bit. A summer or so before, we had let James Blackwood's youngest son, Billy, travel with us during summer vacation. He played drums. James had bought him a set of drums when he was fourteen and Billy learned to play them well.

We let him play for the Stamps Quartet at the National Quartet Convention in Memphis one year, and for two summers he traveled with us.

Then, during the summer before his senior year in high school, I persuaded Billy's father to let him go on the road full time with us, taking a correspondence course to finish school. We sold him on the idea and James agreed.

This gave us what I'd been looking for since the younger members of the quartet convinced me that instrumentation would help capture young audiences. We had a full band and eight people on stage—four singers, and four on instruments. The guys were so talented that any time they wanted to, even in the middle of a song, the four singers could switch to the instruments and the instrumentalists to the mikes to sing, and the crowds loved it.

We had great success in attracting young people to our

concerts because, except for me, the Stamps Quartet was among the youngest in the business—and so talented the guys could sing and play anything.

Early in 1968 Mylon left us again and went back with his family singing group, the LeFevres, and Tim Baty, a youngster from Michigan who had been to our school three years, joined us as bass guitarist. Within a short time he developed into a fine bass player, but the army got him just after the National Quartet Convention in 1969.

Jim Hill left late in 1968. Hovie Lister needed a lead singer for the Statesmen to replace Jack Toney, who then stayed out of professional gospel music for twenty years and finally came back with the Stamps Quartet. Jim said he felt he could last longer in the business if he could sing the lead part instead of tenor, so he became a Statesman.

We hired Roy McNeil to replace Jim, and that was a stroke of fortune. Roy had sung with the Rangers Trio, the Prophets Quartet, and the Statesmen for a while. He sang tenor for the Rangers, but had to sing the lead with the Prophets and Statesmen and this, to an extent, had hurt him because he has a true tenor voice, a high, smooth, easy, pleasant voice.

Roy was great for us on the tenor.

At Christmas of 1969, James's boys, Jimmy and Billy, left the Stamps Quartet and joined their daddy with the Blackwood Brothers. James wanted his boys with him, and I didn't blame him. He'd spent most of his time on the road while they were growing up.

We didn't replace Billy with another drummer. We just dropped the drums. And we hired Ed Enoch to replace Jimmy on the baritone. This was also a stroke of fortune and actually began a new era for the Stamps Quartet. Ed and my daughter, Shirley, were courting pretty heavy (they later got married) and Ed was singing with Jake Hess and the Music City Singers. I asked Jake's permission to talk to Ed about coming to the Stamps, and that's how we got our new baritone singer.

Not only did Ed become my son-in-law, he was a fine singer who put a lot of harmony into our songs.

Roy McNeil left and I hired Bill Baize to sing tenor. Originally from Evansville, Indiana, Bill had never sung with anybody but Smitty Gatlin and never did impress me. I kept searching for the right tenor to replace Roy and people would mention Bill Baize and I'd say, "No, man, there's no way," because I remembered him singing some years back and didn't think he'd fit in. But the boys talked me into giving him a tryout and when he came to my apartment and started to sing, he didn't sing half a song before I knew he was the one we needed. He had more appeal in his voice than any tenor I'd heard in years.

About that time, I went on and did something I'd been thinking about for a long time. I hired a bass singer. Now maybe that sounds like a man who always cuts himself shaving, but I had reasons.

First, my work had become so involved that I didn't have time for everything. Once I found out I had so many brains and got to be such a businessman and started taking on all these responsibilities, I began to realize why big businessmen jump out of those forty story buildings. Those things will drive you right up the wall if you don't have time to fool with them. And I didn't.

I ran our publishing companies. At one time I was trying to run a recording company and talent agency from the back of the bus. And for several years, operation of the National Quartet Convention had been my responsibility, and that, in itself, had become a year-round operation. We had a quartet convention office with one girl employed the full year and two others about six months a year. That was how much detail there was to running the convention.

I thought by easing out of a regular singing routine I could devote more time to those business interests.

Another thought crossed my mind, too. I was getting a little age on my shoulders, and those singing audiences dug young singers. I thought I had enough sense to know that even old people like young people and I had no intention of standing up there and singing until people began to say, "I wish he'd shut his mouth and let somebody up there who can sing." That wasn't the way I intended to go out of this business.

Anyway, I hired Richard Sterban to sing bass with the Stamps Quartet, which freed me to do specialty numbers and whatever else I pleased. Richard was singing with the Keystone Quartet and everyone in the Stamps thought he was a good bass singer and a fine fellow.

I'd known Richard a long time. When he was fourteen

and I was singing with the Blackwood Brothers, we played Lancaster, Pennsylvania, and Richard rode a long way to get there. All night long he followed me around like I used to follow Arnold Hyles. Richard finally got up enough nerve to ask me what made me sing so low.

I couldn't think of a thing in particular that made my voice so low, but I was drinking a cup of black coffee when he asked me, and I said, "Drink black coffee, son; don't ever use nothing but black coffee."

Richard told me later that he went home that night and got his mother out of bed to make him a pot of black coffee. He said he drank so much of it he got sick. He hated black coffee, but because of what I told him he drank so much of it he got to liking it. He drinks his coffee black today. Maybe it did help him. He has been singing great bass for the Oak Ridge Boys for more than twenty years.

When I finally got the Stamps Quartet built just like I wanted it, I had to credit the Oak Ridge Boys for lending a hand.

At one time, I was running Sumar Talent Agency and the National Quartet Convention and I put both of these ahead of my quartet. I got so involved with them I couldn't see it was hurting the quartet. After we formed "Gospel Festival, U.S.A." with the Oak Ridge Boys and Singing Rambos, I began to see what I had done.

We played town after town with the Oaks and Rambos and it got so the Oaks were putting it to us every night. Just as sure as we got to a concert they'd plaster us good. When you work with the same groups every night and one is putting it to you night after night, you'll do one of two things: you'll either get on the ball, or you'll get out.

Well, I went to work. I turned all the Sumar business over to John Matthews and began concentrating on improving the Stamps Quartet. We practiced until we had songs running out our ears. We worked new material into the act. We did everything we knew to improve ourselves, and pretty soon we were to the point that we could lay it on the Oak Ridge Boys once in a while. We continued to improve, and it made the Oaks work harder. I'm not saying that our quartet became better than theirs. I'm saying that any time we put it to them three nights in a row, you'd find them in the woodshed rehearsing. They were as competitive a group as I had ever seen.

The competition between the Stamps and the Oaks made both quartets better. This was one thing that built the Blackwood-Statesmen team. Working together night after night, any time one quartet sat down and the other laid it on them, they'd go back to work and improve themselves.

That's what happened to us, and I personally thanked the fellows in the Oak Ridge Boys for waking us up and putting us to work. The Stamps Quartet reached the point, with or without me, that it held its own with any quartet in gospel music. I made Ed Enoch manager and he handled all the business for the Stamps. The boys played a lot of dates without me, and folks told me that they missed me, but that they enjoyed the quartet. That made me feel good. That was what I'd been trying to accomplish.

*   *   *

With all its youth, the Stamps Quartet was a fun group. We had fun on the bus, at work, in concert, anywhere we were. Being associated with those young men meant much to me.

More than anything else, however, we enjoyed sending crowds home happy and we constantly strove to improve our stage performances, to make them more tuneful, and when the occasion called for it, funnier.

I learned, the same as James Blackwood learned long before that, to seize any opportunity for clean comedy on the stage and capitalize on it.

One November the Stamps Quartet sang in Long Beach, California, on a program with the Imperials and McDuff Brothers. Long Beach was a favorite stop for the Blackwood Brothers and Statesmen, who always go over big out there.

The master of ceremonies that night was an Assembly of God preacher. He had been told to build up the next date for the Long Beach Auditorium, which would be January eighteenth, when the Stamps Quartet would be back, along with the Statesmen and Blackwood Brothers.

The promoter wanted to make certain that the date, January eighteenth, was drilled into the heads of the audience.

There had been some foul-up in publicizing dates and this preacher was instructed to emphasize January eighteenth.

He chose to do it this way: "Ladies and gentlemen, we will have another sing here on January eighteenth—if Jesus doesn't come between now and then."

The McDuff Brothers sang, and the preacher came back out to introduce another group. Before bringing them on, he said, "The only thing that will stop us from having a sing here January eighteenth is if Jesus comes."

When that group finished, the preacher returned to introduce me. I was to bring on the Imperials.

The preacher's words were still ringing in the audience's ears when I stepped to the mike. I stood a minute and gauged that Southern California crowd of fifty-five hundred people as being in a good mood, and suddenly the words I wanted came to me.

"Ladies and gentlemen," I said, "you have heard the good preacher say that if Jesus comes we won't have a sing here January eighteenth.

"Now, I'm not trying to tend to His business, but I think I know this area well enough to say that if Jesus does come, there'll be enough people left to fill this auditorium."

Well, that was one on the audience, and it let out a howl.

When the laughter subsided, I had another inspiration. "Another thing," I said to the audience. "Regardless of what happens between now and then, on January eighteenth, Brother Hovie Lister and the Statesmen Quartet will be here, too."

The audience came unglued at that, and we were all so relaxed after that, audience and performers both, that we had one of the finest concerts I've ever taken part in.

*   *   *

The quickest thing that will kill a quartet is negativism. I have never allowed anyone in the Stamps Quartet to get by with a negative attitude—complaining, grousing, finding fault with everything. There is no place for that.

The more negative you are, even on your best programs, will make fifteen minutes seem like an hour. But if you go on stage with a positive attitude an hour will seem like fifteen minutes. Since I took over the Stamps Quartet, I doubt if the boys have ever done five shows with a negative attitude. I simply won't allow it.

We take such a positive approach that we sometimes do our best programs for some of our smallest crowds.

Once we were in a church in Flagstaff, Arizona, and had about forty people. I had booked it because we needed a place to stop and sing on a long trip from Amarillo, Texas, to Phoenix. I had Donnie Sumner, Jimmy Blackwood, and Jim Hill in the quartet.

The crowd was a bit on the dead side that night and just couldn't or wouldn't get into the program and this had a negative effect on the quartet, especially on Jim Hill. But I was determined to give those forty people a good program.

At intermission, I went out to our record table and got a songbook and turned down about thirty songs that featured Jim. Starting the last half of the program, I began to call the songs I'd singled out. I would sing the verses and let the quartet have the choruses and that's where Jim took over. As we went along, after every song, Jim would back up and bow and say to me, "J. D., you're killing me."

I said, "You sing like you're supposed to sing and we'll quit."

We sang for two hours on that last half and both Jim and the crowd got into the spirit of the thing and we had such a good time and did such a good job that the church gave us a check for $250. This was in the late sixties when our flat rate was somewhere between $300 and $400.

A positive attitude pays off in more ways than one.

Also, you never know who's in a small audience. John Matthews booked us into what we thought was a church in Grant's Pass, Oregon, one time, and it turned out to be an old house. A preacher had started his own church in that house and picked out the biggest room to be his sanctuary. We set up our sound system in that room, and I had never seen such a sad place to sing in. Donnie, Jimmy, and Mylon LeFevre were in the quartet at that time, and they were all kids. They had never had to sing in a room like that, not with the Stamps Quartet, and when we started singing they began to giggle and snicker and I turned around and chewed them out in front of the audience.

There was a man in the audience who had come out just to see if J. D. Sumner and the Stamps Quartet really were appearing in that little church. He came in late, and when he saw it was actually us, he went to a phone and called his pastor and said, "It is J. D. Sumner and the Stamps. You ought to come over here and see this." The pastor came and enjoyed it so much he started booking us in the Second Baptist Church of Grant's Pass, where he was the pastor, and it became one of our best West Coast dates.

You never know who's there. That's one reason the Stamps Quartet will knock itself out to entertain forty people just as much as to entertain 4,000.

CHAPTER NINETEEN

Gremlins and Hecklers

In our business we aren't faced with as many hecklers as entertainers in other fields, but we have an occasional one. Gremlins are what we have to look out for. They can strike at any time, but mostly they wait until you get on stage before a large crowd.

A few years ago the Stamps Quartet, Blackwood Brothers, Statesmen, and the Rebels were singing in Chicago. John Hall had recently left the Blackwood Brothers to go into evangelistic work, and London Parris had come over from the Rebels to sing bass for the Blackwoods. St. John Gresham had taken London's place with the Rebels.

One thing those two bass singers have in common is that Lee Roy Abernathy, who went in for unusual names, named them both. London's real name was Conley Parris, but when he got a job singing with the Homeland Harmony years ago, Lee Roy renamed him London to go with Parris, giving his name a European ring. When John Gresham replaced London with the Rebels, Lee Roy, then playing piano for the Rebels, dreamed up the "Saint" to go before his name: St. John Gresham. In recent years, though, Gresham dropped the "Saint" and reverted back to his real name.

Neither had sung previously in Chicago with the quartets they were then with, and this was a good night to show them off. There were five thousand people in the auditorium.

Almost every song both quartets sang had a good bass lead, and both of those guys dragged bottom that evening. They put on a good show.

I have never had trouble keeping up with any bass singer

151

when it came to digging a little deeper, but on this night I wasn't in the competition at all. I had been with the Stamps for about three years and had been in Chicago many times previously with both the Stamps and Blackwood Brothers, and I felt that I shouldn't get involved that night. That show belonged to London and St. John. Besides, those people in Chicago knew I could get on down there whenever I wanted to.

The Rebels were on first, then the Blackwood Brothers, then the Stamps, and finally the Statesmen. London made a pretty good hit just before we came on, so I stepped to the mike and said, "This seems to be the night for the Battle of Bass Singers, and I don't want to get into it.

"This old boy singing with the Rebels, St. John Gresham," I said, "is not doing a bad job. In fact, he's a pretty cotton-picking good bass singer, and he's going to be a lot of trouble to a lot of bass singers."

The crowd gave me a hand, for I was patting fellow bass singers on the back.

"When London left the Rebels," I continued, "it didn't ruin them to lose a bass singer they'd had for thirteen years. They're a good quartet still.

"And I'm certainly not trying to tell you that London Parris is not a great bass singer, because he is great. . . ."

They gave London a hand. . . .

". . . but even with his greatness," I continued, "he has some bad points."

That hushed the crowd, which leaned forward eagerly to hear what I would say next.

"When a man is a good man," I said, "and he leaves a quartet, naturally he takes away some assets and he also takes some liabilities . . ."

Now, here I meant to say that London has the worst breath in the business . . . but I was on stage and in the excitement of the moment, what I said was "London Parris has got the worst breast in the business."

That brought down the house. The audience rolled in the aisle, howling. All my boys, with tears streaming down their faces from laughter, got up and walked off stage and left me standing there with my face red as blood, and Hovie Lister finally came to my rescue.

He walked on stage like he was going to say something to the crowd that would pull me out of the hole, but he just grabbed me by the seat of the pants and dragged me backward off the stage.

*   *   *

Gremlins that bring out the wrong words strike everyone sooner or later. The first time one reared up in a situation that affected me was years ago when I was with the Sunshine Boys.

We went to New York for a recording session with Decca and after we finished, Paul Cohen, Decca's A&R man, took us in his office to hear a recording of Red Foley and the Jordanaires doing *Steal Away*. Embarrassing though it was, I sat there and cried in that big New York office.

Red Foley was one of my favorite show people. His narrations used to thrill me to death. I still own every one he made.

Steal Away goes like this: "I was walking in Savannah past a church decayed and dim, and there slowly through the window came a plaintive funeral hymn . . ." and so on.

They gave us a tape of Foley's *Steal Away* and after we left we decided we'd learn it. Thinking it would be better if I didn't do the whole narration, we let Freddie Daniels introduce the song and do the narration to where the old Negro preacher began preaching. When Freddie said, "And he said . . . ," I would come up and begin my part: "Now don't be weeping by this little bit of clay, for the little boy that lived there, he done gone and run away. . . ."

This was one of the most serious numbers we ever did, but one night in Clarksburg, West Virginia, Freddie was hit by that gremlin, and passed it right on down to me. When he started the narration, he was supposed to say, "I was walking in Savannah past a church decayed and dim . . ." but he said, "I was walking in Decatur down Decatur Street . . ." and I thought, "Holy Toledo, how can I be serious when he's got me in Decatur, Georgia, instead of Savannah?"

With that, I went blank, too, and we finally had to apologize and do another song.

*   *   *

Sometimes you can pull out of a hole like that without missing a beat. The Stamps Quartet played a little town in Texas and we were really communicating with the people. I was out in the audience, where I could reach out and touch them, narrating *The Farmer and the Lord*, which was pretty big for me at the time.

Suddenly I went blank. I came to a place where I couldn't think of a thing.

It was a serious moment. The crowd was so quiet you could hear a pin drop, and I thought, "How silly!" and the thought tickled me.

I put my hands over my face and was laughing at myself for being so dumb and the audience thought I was crying. They never knew the difference. Perhaps it was the wrong thing to do, fooling the people, but when you're caught in a trap, you get out any way you can.

It would have been a shame to ruin the narration, so I just laughed silently a minute until I thought of the words, then I went on with it and no one ever knew the difference.

*   *   *

We get some hecklers, too, but you learn early in the game how to handle them.

The Stamps Quartet played a fair in Kenton, Ohio, and had to drive from St. Louis, about five hundred miles away. We left St. Louis at 3:30 in the morning after doing a program there, and had to be in Kenton ready to sing at 1 p.m.

When we pulled into the fair about 12:30 p.m. it was raining. I went to the fair manager who said, "I had intended for you to sing in the open, but we'll have to move into the grandstand."

That presented a problem. The grandstand seats were covered, but the stage wasn't, so we had to set up our mikes in the grandstand seating area.

Because of the rain, which came down so hard it chased everybody inside, we had an overflow crowd of about two thousand. They had no other place to go.

We were in such a position in the grandstand that we could actually touch the people. I walked around and patted the little kids on their heads while we sang.

Soon after we began, an obviously inebriated fellow wobbled in and climbed the grandstand. He passed right beside me and I stuck out the mike trying to get him to sing, but he declined and went on over to his seat and sat down.

After a couple of songs, I turned the program over to Tony and the band to play an instrumental, and the drunk liked it. He dug the jive stuff.

When the band finished, the drunk yelled, "Hey, how about playing a selection!"

"Play a what?" I asked him.

"Play a selection," he said, and his tongue was pretty thick.

"A selection!" I said. "Now, we've had a lot of requests for that and we're trying to get to it. We'll do it as soon as we can."

The audience chuckled and I thought that crack might hold him, and it did for a few minutes, but as I was talking to the audience the drunk got up and came stumbling down through the grandstand.

Again he passed by me, then stopped, turned around and motioned for me to come over. He wanted to say something.

I walked over to him and held the microphone close. He didn't realize he was talking to two thousand people, for he said, "Buddy, I'm not leaving 'cause of you. I gotta go pee."

Believe me, that fellow got the biggest laugh that day. All I could think to say was, "I hope you make it, partner."

CHAPTER TWENTY

Sidelines

I wrote more than five hundred gospel songs, most of them when I was with the Blackwood Brothers and James was furnishing the inspiration—or the goading.

When I wrote songs, I used a rhythm guitar, the only instrument I can play, and I'm not very good with it. I used a Martin guitar, a truly fine instrument.

In writing a song, all I needed was an idea. James gave me a lot of my song titles. The tune was formed by the chord I would play on the guitar, and words were never a problem.

This may not be the way Irving Berlin wrote songs, but it's the way that worked best for me. Every artist has his own pecularities. I read that Thomas Wolfe wrote novels in long-hand on a yellow legal pad on top of a refrigerator, because he was so tall and could think best while standing. And I've read that Ernest Hemingway wrote descriptive stuff in long-hand and conversation on a typewriter because people talk like a typewriter—clackety, clackety, clack.

So I have my own way of songwriting.

The only music I ever studied was in the old-fashioned way. A man would come through the country holding singing schools in churches, teaching singing by shaped notes, which is a pretty easy method to learn. The Rev. Vep Ellis, who wrote many gospel songs, taught me music by that method. I attended several of the ten-night or two-weeks singing schools at our church.

I also learned some music from S. L. Wallace, a writer for the Stamps-Baxter Music Company who went to the same church we did.

I guess I always had a lot of songs in me, but I didn't know how to get them out until I went with the Blackwood Brothers. James seemed to inspire me. He would suggest a title for a song, or a theme for one, or just mention that we ought to have something new about the Jordan River, or something like that, and a song would come to me. I don't know why. He just seemed to be able to draw them out of me.

Like one day we were cruising through Texas, needing a diversion to break the monotony of the bleak landscape. James was driving. He got to thinking about needing a new song and called Wally Varner, Bill Shaw, and me up front; all three of us wrote songs.

"Okay," he said, "we've got three songwriters here. I'm going to give you a title and I want all three to go back to your places and write a song by that title. When you're through, each of you will sing your song and I'll be the judge as to whose song is best. Agreed?"

We agreed.

"The title," he said, "is *On the Other Side of Jordan.*"

We went to work immediately and after a while all came back up front. Cecil was driving by this time and James was relaxing in his reclining chair.

One by one we sang our songs, like three third graders singing for teacher, and James declared me the winner. Not only that, but we took the song I wrote, put it on our programs and recorded it for RCA Victor. Other quartets recorded it, too.

About all I needed was a suggestion, I suppose, and James was a regular suggestion box.

* * *

I think the incident I remember best from my songwriting days was the day I wrote the Hawaiian album that the Blackwood Brothers recorded.

We sang in Long Beach, California, one night and after our performance James went to a Hawaiian restaurant to eat. They had a Hawaiian band that played Aloha music and sang throughout the meal. James was absolutely thrilled with their singing; he thought it was the prettiest music he had ever heard. He also wondered if he could do that kind of singing.

James came to me later that night and asked if I could write something gospel with a Hawaiian flavor and we'd see if he could sing it.

So I wrote the song *Aloha Time.* Jake Hess was on the bus with us that night when I showed the song to James and told him how it went. James sang it so beautifully that Jake remarked, "That's tremendous. I'm glad I know somebody who can do a song like that. It's great."

Certainly James appreciated the compliment, and it probably helped him expand his idea to doing a complete Hawaiian gospel album.

Soon after that, we were riding through Indiana one day and when we reached Terre Haute James had made up his mind that we would do the Hawaiian album. From a pay station he telephoned Darol Rice of RCA Victor and told Darol that he thought it would be good if we recorded a gospel album with Hawaiian sound, using the steel guitar and the mandolin and the works.

You always try to get a different approach for an album to make it sell better, something novel, and apparently James did a good selling job. He came back to the bus and said, "J. D., I want you to write some Hawaiian songs. We're going to cut a Hawaiian album."

We chose *Aloha Time,* two songs that Vep Ellis had written, *Jesus Fills My Every Need* and *I'll be True,* added *Beautiful Isle of Somewhere,* and I was to write the rest.

It's roughly sixty miles from Terre Haute to Indianapolis, and while we traveled those miles I roughed out eight songs with a Hawaiian flavor.

I put down all the words, made notes of chords and when I played and sang them for James later, he liked them. We used all of the songs on the album and every one of them was pretty good.

James has said that this album is his favorite of all the Blackwood Brothers recordings—he really digs Hawaiian music—and a lot of other people felt the same way. We entitled the album *Beautiful Isle of Somewhere* and it became the third best selling album the Blackwood Brothers ever did.

I wrote a lot of different type songs—like those Hawaiian numbers. I wrote spirituals like *He's All That I Need* and *Crossing Chilly Jordan,* sentimental tunes like *When I'm*

Alone and *Behind Your Tears,* and rousers like *Walking and Talking with My Lord* and *He Means All the World to Me,* but I suppose the most popular song I wrote was *The Old Country Church.*

I wrote it from a suggestion, too, but not from James. We were singing in the Coliseum in Montgomery, Alabama, one Sunday afternoon and an elderly gentleman came to me and said, "I wish you all would sing some of the songs that I sang in church when I was a boy."

I thought about it a while, wrote some verses, and when we returned home I picked choruses from several old songs like *In the Sweet By And By, Shall We Gather at the River, Leaning on the Everlasting Arm,* and *I'm Redeemed,* and put them with the verses.

I worked on the song for a day or two and approached James as we were leaving Indianapolis for Dayton, Ohio, a few nights later. I got out my guitar and sang *The Old Country Church* for the quartet on the bus, and James was so taken with it that he did something in Dayton that he had never done before. He asked me for the song and I gave him the piece of paper that I'd scribbled the words on.

The house was packed with people and James told them that I had written a song that we hadn't learned yet, but we would sing it from the piece of paper and see if the crowd liked it.

So we sang *The Old Country Church* for the first time in public and the audience applauded loudly. We sang it again and again and the crowd kept asking for more.

We knew at that moment that it would be a hit, and from there on it became one of the biggest hits the Blackwood Brothers ever had.

In fact, the night we recorded our *On Tour* album in Municipal Auditorium in Long Beach, California, with five thousand people on hand, we sang *The Old Country Church* and the audience made us repeat it several times, and the Statesmen came out and joined us and we sang it several times more.

Because of that one song, I think, that album became one of our best sellers.

* * *

I wrote so many songs that I can't remember all of them. Once I was riding with the Imperials on their bus and they were practicing a song entitled *Somebody Pray for Me.*

I listened a while, and said, "Man, that's a good song. Whose is it?"

They stopped singing and looked at me like I was a fool. "Are you crazy?" Joe Moscheo asked. "You wrote it."

Until Joe reminded me I honestly didn't remember writing the song, but I liked it so well that second time around that the Stamps Quartet recorded it on our next album.

* * *

I haven't written a good song in ten years. It is my belief that a songwriter has only so many songs in him, and when he writes them, his songwriting days are basically over. That was true of Albert E. Brumley, who probably wrote more popular songs that were recorded than any other person in our business. He wrote *Turn Your Radio On, I'll Fly Away, I'll Meet You in the Morning, If We Never Meet Again*—just hundreds and hundreds of great songs, but in his last years he never wrote anything worth a dime. Bill Gaither has already quit writing. He wrote some great songs. I'm not saying he has used up his talent, but everything he had in him apparently has come out. Dottie Rambo was the same way. So was Big Chief. And I am certainly paddling that same canoe. Because I can't write songs to measure up to what I wrote in the old days, I just refuse to write and make a fool of myself. Songwriters burn themselves out.

If you want to know the truth about it, nobody is writing consistently good songs any more. Once in a while one comes up, like when the Kingsmen found *Wish You Were Here.* That's a beautiful song. And Gold City ran across one, *Midnight Cry.* That was a fantastic song.

There just aren't many talented songwriters around today. Songwriting is a dying art, and if something isn't done it'll be gone.

* * *

Another way I learned to make money years ago was by doing commercials. Remember those "Otto the Orkin Man" commercials? They were in use for twenty years or more. That was Old J. D. doing the Orkin Man. I cut those commercials in Atlanta in 1952 and they survived longer, I guess, than most other commercials.

* * *

I ran the Stamps School of Music each June in Waxahachie, Texas, but we didn't do it as much to make money as to further gospel singing.

Over the long haul, we lost money in the school and in others we conducted, too, but the value of the school to gospel music couldn't be measured in dollars and cents.

The school attracted singers from all over the country. We couldn't begin to count the graduates of the Stamps School of Music who became headliners in gospel music.

Hovie Lister, Terry Blackwood, Cecil Blackwood, Glen Payne, Tim Baty, Dave Hildreth, Tony Brown, Jimmy Blackwood, Roger Wilde, Larry Orrell, the Goss brothers, all were products of the Stamps School of Music. The list could go on and on.

There was a reason for having such a school. Gospel music is Southern oriented, although it has now spread all across the nation, and basically gospel music uses shaped notes while all other music uses round notes.

The shaped note music we taught at the Stamps School was really a shorthand method of learning how to read music, and we had a shorthand method of teaching.

You couldn't begin to go through any other school of music, where round notes are taught, and learn to read music in three weeks. It would take you almost that long to get enrolled.

In our school we had three weeks to get the job done, and we could teach a person in that time to sing by shaped notes.

We used the same methods that were employed in the ten-night singing schools of the 1930s and 1940s.

But where our method has assets, it also has liabilities: You can't learn by our method and then read music written in round notes—without extensive study, of course.

We teach that the shape of a note gives it a certain sound, like *do* (pronounced *dough*) has one sound, *re* has another, *mi* still another, and so on.

Ear training is as important as anything else in singing by shaped notes.

We feel gospel music as we know it would eventually die out, or at least be swallowed up, if it weren't for the Stamps school. There wouldn't be any other place a person could learn to sing by shaped notes. All of this, of course, originated back in the old days when there were men who would go around to churches and schoolhouses and teach those ten-night singing schools. That isn't done any more. What Frank and V. O. Stamps did was take this method of teaching and put it in the Stamps School of Music.

When we bought Frank Stamps out he said he didn't especially care if we didn't continue to put out convention books, but he wanted us to keep the school going.

You can't operate such a school without getting it in your blood and without seeing the real reason for it.

I had to drop the Stamps School of Music in the early 1970s when the Stamps Quartet began singing backup for Elvis Presley. It seemed that every time we scheduled the school Elvis had a tour, and since I couldn't do justice to both, I cancelled out the school.

*   *   *

Many of the more successful gospel singers go into the recording end of this business, not cutting records but producing them.

Up to and through the 1950s we left recording to the recording companies, Decca, RCA Victor, Capitol, and so on. But about 1960, when the Statesmen-Blackwood Brothers team was at its peak, we started a recording company of our own. We talked it over and planned it as a joint venture between the two quartets.

Wally Varner came up with the name of Skylite Recording Company and we chartered it. Jake Hess and I were put in charge of the operation.

The Speer Family was the first to record with us. We then turned out some Blackwood Brothers and Statesmen records, though we were allowed to record only those songs that had previously been recorded on other labels. Both quartets were under contract to RCA at the time. Even with this restriction, we were able to get a few quality albums on the market.

After that, we began to record the Oak Ridge Boys, Florida Boys, Blue Ridge Quartet, Harmoneers, and the Harvesters.

We recorded about every top quartet in the business because we were the first such label to be organized within the industry itself.

The LeFevres of Atlanta started their recording operation, Sing Recording Company, about the time we started Skylite, and they had the Prophets and Blue Ridge, for whom we also cut records, the Johnson Sisters, and the LeFevres with Jimmy and Rex.

Soon after that, John T. Benson started the Heart Warming label.

With all of us in it, the recording business became a competitive thing, and soon it began to take too much of our time.

The Statesmen and Blackwood Brothers turned over the sole responsibility of running Skylite Recording Company to me, and it required too much of my time and became too complicated a venture.

I was on the road most of the time. We had purchased the James D. Vaughan Music Company and I was running it, and on the strength of Skylite's success, we started the *Singing Time in Dixie* television series.

Before long, I had more than I could do, and I began to talk to our partners about selling Skylite.

We found a buyer, a group of businessmen in Cleveland, Tennessee, and sold the company.

The Stamps Quartet remained on the Skylite label for a while, then switched to Heart Warming. Bob MacKenzie, who produced Heart Warming recordings, was the best in the business, and I think the albums we cut with Heart Warming substantiated that.

* * *

Perhaps the biggest venture I ever engaged in was the one that organized the Sumar Talent Agency.

Jake Hess was the first to go into this type of business. He started what he called Pete Emory Productions and booked the Stamps Quartet and the Imperials.

Don Light also started a talent agency in Nashville about that time and became very successful with it.

After Jake had his heart attack and was forced to cut down on his activities, he dropped his agency, and I began to think about creating one.

I talked over the idea with James Blackwood and decided to go ahead.

I arrived at the name Sumar by taking the MAR from my wife's name, Mary, and the SU from our last name, Sumner, reversing them and putting them together as SUMAR.

At the 1968 National Quartet Convention—another of my babies, by the way—Sumar became a reality. We hired John Matthews, who had managed the Rebels Quartet for twenty years, and put him in charge of Sumar's booking operations. He moved from Florida to Nashville and went to work with a firm hand.

We bought an old house on 17th Avenue South in Nashville and moved our businesses into it: our offices, Sumar Talent Agency, music companies, and some other things.

I must admit that we had some appealing talent from the start, which was one of the reasons Sumar leapt off the ground so quickly. We signed the Blackwood Brothers, the Statesmen, the Stamps Quartet, the Prophets, and the Kingsmen.

Later, we added the Dixie Echoes, the Imperials, the Klaudt Indian Family, the Downings, the Speer Family, the Weatherford Quartet, the Singing Hemphills, the Trav'lers, and the Gospel Harmony Boys.

We had a complete management contract with the Imperials, who were honored at the first annual Dove Awards Banquet in Memphis in October, 1969, as the best quartet in gospel music.

The Imperials became our hottest and most complex commodity. They moved into what I called domestic bookings, backing both Elvis Presley and Jimmy Dean in stage shows, fairs, television appearances, and such. They played Las Vegas regularly with Dean and Presley.

Through Sumar, the Imperials were booked on the Tonight Show, Merv Griffin Show, Joey Bishop Show, Mike Douglas Show, and other network productions.

They recorded the theme song for the Daniel Boone television show.

Talent agencies added a tremendous growth to our business. For a quartet, affiliation with a talent agency became a valuable instrument. If a promoter called us and wanted to book the Blackwood Brothers for a certain date, and they were already booked for that date, we would suggest another quartet from our agency, and a lot of quartets got lucrative bookings this way. If that promoter had been forced to make fifteen telephone calls to find a quartet with that particular date open, he might give up and cancel the date altogether. Promoters learned that they could fill entire dates with one telephone call to our agency.

Many of the agencies worked together. When a promoter called an agency to book talent on a certain date and all that agency's groups were already booked, the agency would phone other agencies to see who they had open on that date. It was a cooperative thing.

Alas, I finally had to close Sumar's doors, not because of a lack of cooperation from promoters, but from the quartets themselves. We were booking good dates for all, but all weren't paying our commission, and a talent agency operates on commissions from its groups.

After a few years, Sumar slipped so far in the red we just closed the books and let it die.

But the idea was sound, and those talent agencies prospered which had the time to pay a hundred percent attention to their business. Few major groups today work without the help of an agency.

* * *

Another of my ideas, of which I am extremely proud, produced the National Quartet Convention. This idea was fostered many years ago. When I was with the Sunshine Boys, I tried to sell Wally Fowler on the notion that we have one time a year when we could get all gospel musicians together for two or three days in the same town. Wally considered it, but apparently thought it too much a gamble to risk the money it would involve.

Then I came to the Blackwood Brothers, and James was the type of guy who would consider any good idea. So as soon as I got us a new sound system and a bus, I started pushing the idea of a National Quartet Convention.

The idea stemmed originally from the camp meetings we used to attend in Florida. Camp meetings were based on preaching, of course, but I couldn't understand why we couldn't do the same thing with singing.

I sold James, and in 1956 we held the first National Quartet

Convention in Memphis. We chose Memphis because that's where we lived and it seemed as central a point as any other. Too, it had good facilities.

The first convention was a success. The second convention was also successful.

Then we moved it to Birmingham in 1958 and to Atlanta in 1959, thinking it would be a better convention if we moved it from town to town each year. But in Birmingham, attendance dropped off, and in Atlanta it was even worse.

The 1960 convention was moved back to Memphis where it remained until 1971, and each convention got bigger and better than the preceding one.

We moved it to Nashville in 1971. Nashville had become the headquarters of gospel music, like country music. It was where the agencies were, where the recording companies were, where many of the quartets lived, where the Gospel Music Association and the Hall of Fame were located, and it was more centered than Memphis in the heart of the good gospel music country. We felt the convention would grow greater and mean more to everyone if it were permanently located in Nashville.

Since the convention was my idea to begin with, James gave me the authority to make major decisions, and I operated it like I thought it should be run.

Our first convention was a three-day affair. Thursday night fell flat, but Friday and Saturday were successful. The next year I picked out four of the top groups of the day—the Blackwood Brothers, Statesmen, Speer Family, and Le-Fevres—and let them sing in a special Thursday night concert. Attendance picked up.

The convention went over so well after we moved it back to Memphis that we made it a four-day event, and then a five-day affair. By then we were drawing more people on Wednesday and Thursday nights than we previously had for the entire convention.

We had hopes that within a few years the convention would run a week—and it does today.

When I ran the convention, ninety-eight percent of the groups were professional. Amateurs were allowed only in the talent contest, not on the convention program.

The convention became exactly what I dreamed it would

be, though probably on a larger scale than I had dared imagine. It was a place where singers and fans could mix and mingle. Promoters used it for booking purposes, and some filled all their dates for the following year at the convention. The Gospel Music Association used it for its annual meetings, and in 1969, for the first time, the Dove Awards Banquet, which was then gospel music's equivalent of the Oscar and Emmy presentations, was held during the convention and was a tremendous success.

Finally I had to get out of the convention. It became too much for one man to handle, and I had other fish I wanted to fry.

I enjoyed running the convention, even if it was a mountain of work. We paid the best money many of the groups could earn, and at convention time I had a world of friends.

I ran the convention for the good of the gospel music industry. When Wendy Bagwell and the Sunliters started singing, I offered them $250 to sing at the convention and old Wendy fell all over himself accepting. We had a good convention, so I doubled his pay and gave him $500. Boy, did he leave there walking on air!

I never made any money off the convention. Maybe I was dumb, because there's a lot of money made off it now, but I ran it for the good of the business.

Every group wanted a featured spot on the convention program because most of the promoters and industry people were there. Too, the convention was the Big Daddy of all gospel promotions. Anybody who was anybody was there. I always kept track of who sang where on each program, and if a major group had a bad spot this year, I would see that it had a good, featured place next year.

Les Beasley and the Florida Boys had a bad spot one year, and by an oversight on my part they drew another bad spot the next year, even though I had given Les my word they would have a featured place.

Les is a very open man. You always know what he's thinking because he'll tell you. He came to me on Saturday night and said, "J. D., you lied to me. You told me I'd have a good spot on the convention. I've gotta be in Tampa tomorrow night, and I'm on here after midnight tonight. I can't make my date tomorrow. I booked the date in Florida because I depended on what you told me last year. You've always treated me right, but this time is different. You've rooked me."

He was right, and I knew it. I said, "Well, uh, what would you say if I were to pay you for tonight and let you go right now? Would that make you happy?"

"Yes," Les said, and he chuckled.

"Well, that's fantastic, Les," I said, "because you'll be happy, I'll be happy, and all the people here will be happy because they didn't want to hear you sing anyway. So everybody will be happy."

I wrote him a check and he left laughing.

That's the way I ran the convention, in a way that was good for the entire business.

I remember hiring the Happy Goodman Family once when they first got started—again. Sam Goodman came to me and said they were starting back again and they would like to work at the convention, so I hired them for $250 and paid them $500.

James and Cecil and I owned the convention, and the time came when I bought Cecil's part of everything we were in together. I paid him $40,000, but we forgot to include the convention in the deal. Later, Cecil wrote me that he was taking over the convention because he and James owned two-thirds of it. He wrote that he would hire the groups and decide what every group would be paid, and that he was going to have fifteen minutes of preaching each night of the convention and that every quartet member at the convention would be required to attend the preaching service.

He also wrote that quartets would be permitted to plug records from stage—something I had strictly forbidden.

I wrote Cecil back and made my message very clear: "Until I'm out, I will continue to run the convention, and we will continue to run it on a professional level. We will not plug records from stage; we will not go through the audience selling our wares; and we will not have fifteen minutes of preaching." I finished the letter: "So until you get ready to buy me out, then I will run the convention and run it the way I have always run it."

Cecil had just bought a new bus by solicitation of audiences, and in my letter I jabbed him a little for that. "By the way," I wrote, "I've got two buses, and I bought both of mine. I didn't ask the people to buy them." It was just that type of thing that I thought turned many people off. I didn't believe it was the right way to go—and I still don't.

Cecil got J. G. Whitfield to buy me out with an offer that I could hardly refuse. The convention then encountered financial trouble and J. G., who is a good man, sold it to the present owners.

The convention today is much, much too large for one man to run, like I did in the old days. If I were still running it, it wouldn't be so big. I'm sorry to say that there aren't ten groups in the business today who are truly professional. Most of the groups that sing on the convention today couldn't qualify under the rules we went by. But there were many more professional groups then.

Ours is no longer a quartet business. There are ten mixed groups, maybe fifty, for every good male quartet, and that's too bad. It's changed the business altogether from what it was intended to be.

We have always had female singers—Eva Mae LeFevre, the Speer girls, the Chuck Wagon Gang girls (all of whom go back to the 1930s)—but the one woman who could truly sing with a quartet was Lily Fern Weatherford, because she always sounded like a male tenor. She sang a part in the Weatherford Quartet and if you were listening to one of their records and somebody didn't tell you she was a woman, you wouldn't know it.

The business has changed so much that ninety-five percent of the so-called singers working today are mixed groups. I find nothing wrong with them if that's what the people want to hear, but I'm afraid we've chased more people away from our concerts than we attract.

*   *   *

Most of my efforts have always been directed toward things in gospel music, but I have one hobby that has nothing to do with music. I play golf.

I play golf for fellowship, relaxation, and enjoyment. I really don't work too hard at improving my game; it's just a hobby. But I play well enough to get by.

My best score was a 78 which I shot at Harpeth Hills Golf Course in Nashville.

I keep my clubs on the bus and play every chance I get. I have played golf in every section of the United States and in Mexico and Canada.

One of the greatest thrills of my life came on the golf course. We stopped in Charlotte on the morning of July 18, 1969, on the way from Raleigh to Knoxville.

Bill Hefner, now a member of the United States House of Representatives, but then first tenor for the Harvesters Quartet and promoter of gospel sings in Charlotte, took Roy McNeil and me to play golf at a club in Concord, near Charlotte.

On the sixth hole, a 195-yard, par 3, I drove a 4-wood shot across a lake and straight to the pin. The ball carried well, struck the green about six inches above the pin, and spun backward into the cup.

It was the only hole-in-one I ever made, and I've been playing golf since 1952. I was so thrilled that I probably didn't hit the ground the rest of the round.

CHAPTER TWENTY-ONE

Ministering and Entertaining

Gospel singing is a ministry, but not quite like many groups of today try to make it. People like Hovie Lister, an ordained Baptist preacher, James Blackwood, Dottie Rambo, and Eva Mae LeFevre, to name a few, believed as firmly that they were preaching the gospel through song as any minister who ever stood in the pulpit.

I believe that, too, but I have to explain how I believe it. Gospel music was designed by God as a means of reaching the lost. I believe that so deeply that I wouldn't be on the road as much as I am if it were not so.

But professional gospel music is entertainment.

I believe there is a time and place for all things, and I do not believe that the stage of a gospel singing is the place for thunderous sermons and rip-roaring testimonies. That sort of "gospel singing" alienates half the crowd and keeps thousands of people away from our concerts.

We should let the songs minister. They do. People come to hear great singing, and that's what we ought to be giving them, not a few watered-down songs and twenty minutes of fire and brimstone preaching.

I have my own ideas about most things, and I have definite ideas on this subject. I do not think an all-night sing is the place for sermonizing. People who pay for a ticket to a singing pay to hear us sing, not preach.

Church people hear the finest preachers in the best churches in the country. On any night at a gospel sing, they pay to be entertained with good, clean, family-oriented, Christian entertainment through song.

171

If, during the course of our singing, we move someone nearer the Lord, we've accomplished something.

Many folks tell us that our singing has inspired them to become better people. That's great.

We usually have about four hours to sing at the average concert, and if we use thirty minutes for preaching and testifying, in a way we're short changing the crowd.

Our audiences are made up primarily of Christian people who have heard good preaching since they were children. By and large, they are saved people. They choose the night of a gospel sing to hear good singing, and if we don't give them all we can, we're not doing our job.

*   *   *

In the forties, fifties, and sixties, and even through most of the seventies, most quartets were professional singers. About the only one who did a little preaching from stage was Hovie, who did it in a style that made people laugh, more or less, as part of the entertainment. A lot of his preaching was to introduce songs he wanted people to listen to.

Now, for some reason, many singers think to be popular in what they choose to call Southern gospel music, you have to get up there and preach and cry and testify. It is my belief that when a man buys a ticket to get in, you're infringing on that man's rights to try to cram your ideas of salvation down his throat—because you might just be wrong and his own previous beliefs might have been right.

We were called to sing. Jerry Kirksey wrote a column in *The Singing News* in which he said we should all be good singers. If anyone ever starts enforcing that rule, there are going to be a lot of buses for sale. Let's face it, in gospel music today there are very few good singers. It's getting worse and worse. In the heyday of gospel quartet singing, a lot of kids were inspired to sing because of the Blackwood Brothers and Statesmen. They were inspired to sing bass, for instance, by J. D. Sumner, Big Chief, London Parris, Richard Sterban, and others. Unfortunately, there isn't anybody out there now inspiring these kids. Gospel singers don't even think of that any more.

I see gospel music as an art, and I see it fading out fast. I don't see us drawing in sinners any more. We've got a little circle of people that's small and those are the only people we're reaching. And most of them were saved twenty-five years ago. If we keep shrinking that circle, alienating people, gospel music as I enjoyed it from the forties to the seventies will fade into oblivion.

My wife passed away in 1992. She was sick. If I had done the norm, I would have gone on stage every night and got the sympathy of the people—got a lot of them to pray for her, and sold a lot more records.

Mary was oriented to my singing. In the two months she lay ill, I missed only one night singing—and she jumped on me the next morning. "Why didn't you go sing last night?" she asked. I never brought up Mary's illness on stage, not once. I sang to the people who came to hear us; I tried to entertain them, not make them feel sorry for Mary and me and perhaps go home crying.

Her illness was our problem, mine and her's. I didn't need to take my problem to the stage and stack it on top of the problems all those people out there in the audience already had. They didn't buy tickets to hear what tragedy had hit J. D. and Mary Sumner.

It amazes me what some of the groups tell on stage. I knew one quartet that had a bus wreck, tore up the bus, killed somebody, banged up a couple more, and they got on stage telling about that wreck and how good God had been to them. They shouldn't have said anything. They were trying to jerk tears from the audience, perhaps to enhance record sales.

God didn't kill my wife, nor my mother. They both died, but that's still nothing for me to take on stage with me. Those were tragedies that I've had in my family, the same as you've had tragedies in yours, and nobody gets on a stage and tells about yours. Tragedy is life that began happening back when Adam and Eve messed up.

When the Stamps Quartet goes on stage, we try to do our best with good singing, good songs, good arrangements, excitement in our singing, and I try to put a little comedy into the program so the people will leave in a good mood after having been thoroughly entertained.

You can't forget the message of the song. That's what we try to sell to the audience. At an old-timers singing I heard

Earl Weatherford sing *What a Precious Friend Is He,* a song written by Henry Slaughter, and when he finished singing, Earl said, "What else could I add to that song? That song was inspired." He was right. He didn't have to preach about it for twenty minutes. The song said it all. That's what our songs are supposed to say. That's the way we are supposed to reach the people.

In years gone by, when you tuned in a radio program, you heard the Blackwoods, Statesmen, Harmoneers, Blue Ridge, Speer Family, Homeland Harmony, LeFevres, Stamps, Oak Ridge Boys, Florida Boys. Every one of those groups—and the others I didn't mention in that list—had style. You could listen to one of them sing and no one had to announce who they were. You could tell them apart by their sound. You can't do that today. I hear many complaints that disc jockeys don't announce who's singing. No wonder they need for it to be announced—too many groups sound exactly alike, and too many can't sing an arrangement that's worth listening to.

Some of the disc jockeys are beginning to want to testify on the air. In interviews, I don't even like to talk about my wife passing away, because that's a private thing to me. But one DJ was doing an interview with me and asked if I would mind if he prayed for my wife on the air. He was doing an interview with me—not to let the people hear what I had to say, but so his audience could hear him praying for my wife and think, "What a great man he is!" He could have prayed for my wife before or after that program in the secrecy of his closet, where God could have heard him directly, not with a radio audience.

This is what has happened in gospel music. It's not Christian entertainment anymore; it's not singing; it is nothing but who has the best testimony, and this has prompted people to build, create, and memorize testimonies that will sound good from the stage. It's as if they say, "You gotta get out here and hustle to outdo some of these people with their testimonies."

Let the songs minister! What they say will mean a lot more to the people than what we manufacture to testify.

We're talking about what professional gospel music is. Basically, the Stamps Quartet is going back to what I did when I first started in this business. We're singing a lot of songs that are not gospel. In the early days our programs were an hour and fifteen minutes long with no intermission. We opened with fifteen minutes of gospel, then sang fifteen minutes of Western music, then did fifteen minutes of comedy, sang fifteen minutes of pop (*Old Buttermilk Sky*, etc.) and closed out with fifteen more minutes of gospel. On radio we sang all gospel.

The Stamps Quartet is going back to that type of program because variety programs draw people—sinners included.

Too, the word *gospel* has been so maligned in our business that it turns people off. In our business we've tried for years to find another word to substitute for *gospel*. We never mention the word *gospel* on a program, not that we are ashamed of it, but because we wanted to get some listeners in and then surprise them with the message, with songs about Jesus Christ, songs sung professionally.

I am still searching for a word other than *gospel* to describe our music. Contemporary singers call themselves Christian artists. They do not want to be called gospel singers, and there are reasons for it. They are ashamed of us because of the way we conduct ourselves on stage. People like Amy Grant, Sandi Patti, and Larnelle Harris are fine Christian artists, and their music is contemporary. They don't want to be classified with us because of the caterwauling and the false religion that has crept into our business and is destroying it.

At one time, professional gospel quartet singing penetrated every home in America by way of television channels. When I was with the Blackwood Brothers, we were on the Arthur Godfrey Talent Scouts twice and won it both times, the Dave Garroway Show twice, and Tennessee Ernie Ford's show a couple of times. These were network television shows.

When we went on, they weren't worried about us getting up and testifying and scaring their audience half to death. And we had to choose songs back then that were middle-of-the-road, for which we would be condemned by our peers today. We sang things like *Church Twice on Sunday, and Once in the Middle of the Week.* The Blackwood Brothers won Arthur Godfrey's Talent Scouts with *The Man Upstairs* first, and *The Good Book* second. Gospel songs? James got both of them from Kay Starr, the pop singer who gained fame with songs like *Wheel of Fortune.* But the songs fit a gospel quartet, and we sang them for years and our audiences loved them. Those songs got us on network television.

Let a gospel quartet try to get on network TV today and see what happens. You'd be able to hear the network *hee hawing* all the way from New York to Birmingham.

People will say I'm compromising. That's malarky! The compromise works the other way. We compromise ninety-nine percent of the population when we put on a program like groups put on today. You're compromising when you tell an audience if it doesn't believe it the way you believe it, then, my friend, you can go to hell. That's what it amounts to. Anytime anything is presented but love, you're not representing God. I've known some groups to run down the Baptists from stage, and I've known some to run down the Pentecostals. That is not our calling. Our calling is to sing and I don't believe you'll find an inspired gospel song that runs down any denomination.

What I'm saying doesn't blanket everybody in the business, but those it refers to will know it when they read these words.

And if someone doesn't do something to change the course of things, we're all going to be looking for work soon.

Do what, you ask?

I may sound critical at times. I intend to. You may call it what you like, criticism or prattle; I call it good, sound advice, amassed from a half-century of singing the gospel in almost every big city and little hamlet in the country.

Whether we all like it or not, we are in the entertainment business. The most overused word in our business is *ministry*. Again, whether we like it or not, the ministry in our business lies in the songs we sing—and it's a tremendous thing.

All the guys in the Stamps Quartet are Christians, but we count this a business. It's the way we make our living, giving people good, wholesome, Christian entertainment. There is nothing wrong with that.

And while we're singing, any time the Holy Spirit wants to move, we back off and let the Holy Spirit take over. But it's been my theory not to grab the Holy Spirit and say, "You've got to go on stage tonight because we need to sell more records. People think we're so perfect and so inspirational that if *You* don't go on stage with us, we're gonna have to fake *You*."

The Holy Spirit works in our programs a lot of times, but it's real when it does; it's not part of our act.

We don't get on stage and shout and holler. We don't testify and we don't preach, and we don't consider our work to be a ministry. The ministry lies in our singing, and every time I've used the word *ministry* in this book has been in that context.

Some groups get on stage and fake feeling the Holy Spirit. There are people who sing and at certain places in a song, every night they raise their hands and yell, "Praise the Lord!" They're not praising the Lord! They're praising themselves, drawing attention to themselves. It's a choreographed move. I also don't think singers should shout from stage, "Give Jesus a hand!" What they really mean is "Give me a hand for getting Jesus a hand."

Another thing the Stamps Quartet doesn't do is solicit church dates. We work churches, but we do not go to a church and ask, "Would you let us come to your church and sing on a certain date. We're passing through town that day and have the time to sing in your church." They sing for what I call a hate offering and they call a love offering. Yes, we do work churches, but only on a flat rate, and on special occasions like homecoming when a church wants special entertainment. We never ask them to take up a love offering. In the past we've worked churches for offerings, but when I figured out what we were doing we quit it.

There is a way gospel music can make a comeback, but it has to straighten up its act and become professional again. We would have to work like country music people work, just a professional quartet and a show opener. You could take Gold City, the Cathedrals, the Kingsmen, and the Stamps, and a few others, and put them on any show and know that the audience would be entertained. But what happens is that we work with the *what's thats*, the *who's thats*, and the *whom's thats*, and the audience gets forty-five minutes of professional singing and two hours of *who dats*.

Please don't get me wrong. There must be a place for groups to start, and as show openers is the place. When they work their way up to professional stature where they can draw a crowd, then they can get their own show opener and have at it.

Most groups that start out now want to start at the top.

You can't do that. In any business, you have to pay a price before you attain success. Few want to pay the price anymore.

If gospel music would go back to having only those groups on a show that can really sing, we would improve this business enough for other areas of the Christian entertainment world—and even the secular entertainment world—to take notice again. We need to have some regulations. There are groups traveling and singing now who call themselves professional that couldn't have gotten on the talent contest at the quartet convention twenty-five years ago. They're out there by the thousands.

If we ever get back to the top again, we're going to have to straighten up our act.

*   *   *

The biggest part of the time a quartet is on stage, there is a certain communication it should feel with the audience. We in the Stamps Quartet have been trained to try to attain this communication quickly and to hold it until we leave the stage, but, of course, no one can do that every time.

The communication is one of love and feeling between performer and audience. When we communicate, we feel we're really getting the job done. When we don't communicate . . . believe me, you can feel that, too.

We don't judge a stand on stage by the amount of applause we draw, nor by the excitement we create, nor by the number of tapes we sell, but rather by how well we communicate.

Sometimes we sing a song that really communicates but draws little applause. It gets the audience in a certain mood, and you can tell that you're communicating.

There are nights when we communicate and draw little applause because the audience is in such a mood that it wants songs it doesn't have to clap and whistle for. But on those nights, the audience will compliment us more, buy more records, and let us know in many other ways that they sincerely enjoyed the program.

Those nights are deeply satisfying because we know that we are communicating, and that we are entertaining and, yes, ministering through song.

*   *   *

Another way of communicating with an audience is through humor. I've already given my views that a quartet should not take politics, religion, or any social issue to the stage. I don't think that's our responsibility. Some people take the lesbian and gay thing to the stage; some even write songs about it. That's not our problem and it's not up to the entertainer to go on stage and fight that problem. Nor is it up to the entertainer to go on stage and give our views on religion. It's up to us being entertainers to entertain, and when you entertain, comedy becomes a major part of your program. George Younce is good at comedy on stage, but he uses it a little bit different than I do. All of mine is natural from the standpoint that I say what I think. I don't often do comedy routines.

On a recent program, I said that every time I tried to hire Rick Strickland, our new first tenor, that he was pregnant. That just came to my mind. It got a good laugh. Somebody dared me to tell a joke about a talking frog at a concert in Greenville, South Carolina, one night, and it almost brought the house down because the people in the audience could relate the story to me.

It went like this:

An old man found a frog on the floor of his home and picked it up and started shuffling for the door to put it out. But the frog spoke to him and said, "If you kiss me, I will turn into a beautiful maiden and be yours forevermore."

The old man stared at the frog a moment, then slowly made his way toward the door again. The frog spoke a second time: "If you kiss me, I will turn into a beautiful maiden and be yours forevermore."

That time the man put the frog in his shirt pocket, turned around, and headed back the way he had come, and in a muffled voice the frog spoke the third time: "If you kiss me, I will turn into a beautiful maiden and be yours forevermore."

And the old man replied, "At my age, I believe I'd rather have a talking frog."

Comedy helps you forget your problems, and it draws the audience to you. In Hendersonville, North Carolina, recently, we had a lot of comedy in the program, but when we sang *I Can Feel the Touch of His Hand* and *God Shall Wipe Away All Tears*, you could feel the Holy Spirit there. It was so real to me that a time or two I had to quit singing for a moment because I was crying. Charlie Hodge, one of Elvis's stage men, was there, and he told me later, "I ain't no shouter, but I almost had a fit there." No one had said a word about God or about how we should do this or that, but the Holy Spirit was there and He came voluntarily and was very, very real.

I always involve the audience in my comedy. Not long ago, a man stood up in the audience and started talking to us between songs and I chewed him out in good fun, and he ate it up. I delight when a baby starts crying or gooing in the audience. I'll say something like, "Shut up, kid; I'm up here trying to talk and you're upstaging me." That always draws a laugh and it gets the audience in the program.

My voice, being low like it is, has always scared kids if I don't use it with caution. All my nieces and nephews used to cry when I spoke harshly to them.

Once in Oklahoma City, a woman got up while I was talking and started to step out to the aisle, and I said, "Sit back down," and she promptly sat down in this man's lap and then fell to the floor. I thought, Oh, Lord, I've done it now! And I said, "Lady, I'm sorry; I was just cuttin' up with you." If she'd injured herself, she could have sued me big time.

*　　*　　*

Philosophy is a subject I usually leave alone. I have enough to keep me busy without getting involved in a lot of deep thinking.

But I think a lot about the young people coming into our business. They are different today, and I'm not saying they're wrong. Maybe it's just that times have changed so much. I guess youngsters in my day were thought of by our elders as being different, too.

Most young people coming into gospel music today don't have the appreciation for the business that we had. That's because they don't have to struggle like we did to make good. To most young people now, gospel music is a means to an end, a way to attain a good, enjoyable way of life and make good money. To us it was a religion. It was something we lived, ate, and breathed twenty-four hours a day.

Why did Jake and Big Chief steal peaches to keep on singing? Was it because they knew if they kept singing that some day they would become big stars and make big money? No!

It was because they wanted to sing. Because they loved to sing.

Then, young people admired those like the Hyles brothers and others of their cut much more than they do today. We respected them because of their talent, of course, but also because we knew they had been through the mill to get where they were.

Becoming a professional gospel singer was no picnic then. It was a tough road to follow, and you couldn't even get on the road until you had learned to sing well.

When I came into the business I had one suit—that old sharkskin job with the seat of the pants ripped—but I had to tape up the tear and wear the suit because it was all I had.

We rode in automobiles that we hoped would get us there. We never knew. Often they didn't, and sometimes we had to repair them ourselves. When we got hot, we rolled down the windows; there was no such thing as air conditioning in automobiles then. We rode cramped and slept sitting up, if we slept at all.

Today there are really no rough spots for young singers. They join a quartet which is doing pretty well and right off they're in the high cotton bracket.

Maybe that's the way it's supposed to be: one group pays the price for all who follow. Jesus did that, didn't he? He paid the price for all of us who follow him.

In the Stamps Quartet, we have as many as fifteen different uniforms for stage appearances, we ride in an air-conditioned bus that contains soft chairs, good beds, all the comforts of home.

We have television on the bus—and when you have TV, what more do you need?

And the boys start making good, livable salaries right quickly.

I can tell you, there's a difference—a big difference.

* * *

We went through a period in which great advances were made in instrumentation.

In my mother's day, the only instrument they had was the pump organ. When I came along, the primary instrument was the piano. There was a time between the pump organ and the piano when a guitar—just a plain, old guitar—was the best instrument because it was easiest to carry around. The Blackwood Brothers started out in 1934 using a striped pumpkin-shaped guitar and didn't use a piano until 1938.

But instruments of all sorts were introduced into gospel music in the 1960s—electric guitars, bass guitars, trumpets, drums, tamborines, even fiddles and banjos, and accordions, too.

Handled properly, instruments are fantastic; wrongly used, they're bad news.

In the Stamps Quartet we tried to use instruments right, and we think we did. People told us they enjoyed our music.

Regardless, my views were that young people could be reached through instrumentation, and that was something we tried to do: reach the nation's youth.

Youngsters were responsible for bringing all those instruments into our business. If it had been left to James Blackwood, Hovie Lister, J. D. Sumner, and others like us, I suppose we would still be using the piano and nothing else, because that's what we were used to when we were young, and it was all we needed. The people wanted to hear voices singing, not strings twanging.

But the kids of the sixties and seventies wanted "up tempo" and if we didn't give it to them, they'd go somewhere else and find it. We didn't have enough young people interested in gospel music that we could afford to lose any of them. We needed more. We need more today.

People thought I had ideas years ago of expanding instrumentation with the Blackwood Brothers but couldn't because the guys objected. That was not true. I didn't try to instrumentalize the Blackwood Brothers.

The youngsters I hired into the Stamps Quartet inspired me to form the band we had. They were the ones who wanted to do it, and I just went along with them. Before that, I hadn't given much thought one way or the other to instrumentation.

But I learned the trait of patience from James Blackwood years ago. I learned to listen when someone came up with an idea, and to give it every consideration.

If James hadn't been that way, where would I be today?

No, the instruments weren't my idea, but I'm glad the boys

thought of them. They gave us a better sound, which was one of our primary goals.

A trend like that catches on. Many other quartets went to four-piece bands. Even the Blackwood Brothers went all the way with instruments, and their sound was good.

Since then, the trend reversed itself. Possibly rising expenses had something to do with the obliteration of the band. Few quartets use a full band today. The Kingsmen are an exception. We in the Stamps Quartet have gone to these exotic computerized instruments that mimic an entire band with strings. They are great, properly handled, as C. J. Almgren handles ours.

* * *

Young people have done tremendous things for our business and they'll do great things for the world, if we'll let them. They're honest; they're legit. I believe the young people will get us from religion to real salvation.

Youngsters have their own thing—like long hair. It isn't such a fetish with them as it was a few years ago. They don't try to be ridiculous with it. I don't go for shoulder-length hair, but I've seldom seen a gospel quartet wearing hair that long. Some of the quartets were criticized for wearing long hair, but that was the youth movement in gospel music. Older people made too much to-do about long hair when it became stylish. They put a barrier between long hair and Christianity, but I think the two have nothing to do with each other. Burl Strevel summed it up pretty well when he said, "Show me a barber who can cut my hair and send me to heaven and I'll have my hair cut every day."

One winter morning in Grant's Pass, Oregon, I was feeling pretty blue. That was the morning I wrote the song *I Can Feel the Touch of His Hand.* I went down to the First Baptist Church and met the pastor and we went down to the basement of the church where there were a bunch of young kids shooting pool and throwing darts. They had a big fire going, and were having fun. We joined them for a couple of hours. Later that night in concert at that church, I saw the first four rows filled with those kids in their blue jeans. They were relaxed and they were worshipping. That really sold me on

this concept of the church. You could tell those young people
were evermore Christians.

*   *   *

The one item in our business that a lot of people find hard
to take is the travel, those endless days and long, weary nights
on the road.

I have never found travel too trying. I look forward to
playing new towns and meeting new friends. The only time
I find travel tiresome is on the tail end of a month-long trip,
and then the feeling is only momentary.

Toward the end of a long trip, I'll begin to get weary, but
usually I face each trip with an eagerness usually found in
the most youthful in this business. Every night produces something new and every day becomes a challenge.

Gospel singing is no place for a homebody. During a recent
month, the Stamps Quartet played in seventeen states: Mississippi, Kentucky, Oklahoma, Texas, Arkansas, Maine, Massa-
chusetts, New Hampshire, New Jersey, New York, Arizona,
California, North Carolina, Georgia, Ohio, Pennsylvania,
and Indiana.

That's traveling, brother! Some of our overnight hops would
make Greyhound envious.

We had three overnight trips that month that sound impossi-
ble. On a Sunday we sang in Little Rock, Arkansas, and on
Monday in Holton, Maine. A week later, we jumped from
Kenona, New York, on Tuesday and sang in Tucson, Arizona,
on Thursday. We needed an extra day for that trip. But coming
back from the West Coast the following week, we were in
Wichita Falls, Texas, one night and Winston-Salem, North
Carolina, the next.

We once had an overnight trip from Grand Rapids, Michigan, to Greensboro, North Carolina, and another from Jack-
son, Michigan, to Jacksonville, Florida.

Even with our buses, we couldn't have made trips like those
before interstates. The interstate highway system makes it possible today. This network of four-lane roads will get a quartet
from here to yonder in the quickest possible time short of air
travel.

Because of our fast travel and the access to all places given
us by America's fantastic road system, we not only are able

to play such cities as Atlanta, Detroit, Los Angeles, and Washington, D. C., but also such towns in between as Sylva, North Carolina; Washington Courthouse, Ohio; Oliver Springs, Tennessee; and Sabetha, Kansas.

In gospel music, I am proud to say, we give people in Sylva as fine a show as those in Los Angeles. That's the nature of our business and the people who make it up.

And, I might add, a gospel sing in Sylva will sometimes draw as many or more as one in Detroit. That, I suppose, is the nature of the gospel singing fan; he follows the circuit.

CHAPTER TWENTY-TWO

Elvis Again

B_y 1971 I had the Stamps Quartet where I wanted it. Bill Baize was singing tenor, Donnie Sumner the lead, Ed Enoch baritone, and Richard Sterban bass. Nick Bruno was our pianist. I sang three or four songs on a show, but was content to let Richard sing the bass.

That version of the Stamps had the finest harmony I have ever heard. There wasn't a quartet in the business that could hold a light to us.

I still had Sumar and one of my groups was the Imperials, who sang backup for both Elvis Presley and Jimmy Dean. They were that good.

In November of that year, the inevitable happened. Elvis and Jimmy scheduled simultaneous tours and the Imperials couldn't back both of them. Joe Moscheo was managing the Imperials and his first allegiance was to Jimmy Dean. Possibly he was a bit scared for the Stamps to back up Elvis. He knew of my friendship with Elvis through the years, and he certainly knew what a good quartet we had.

Elvis was scrambling to find another backup group. Moscheo tried to get a Canadian group he knew but they couldn't come. Elvis had Charlie Hodge, his personal aide, to investigate the possibility of getting Jake Hess, Jim Hamill, Herman Harper, and Cat Freeman to back him on this tour, but Charlie had a better idea.

"Before we do that," he told Elvis, "let me call J. D. and see if he has another quartet that might fill in. He's got a talent agency and might have somebody available."

When Charlie called, I said, "Funny you should call be-

186

cause I do have a quartet that's capable of handling that job. I'll send the Stamps Quartet."

I sent our latest recording to Charlie, who passed it on to Elvis. Charlie told me that Elvis played that record over and over for twenty-four hours and then said, "Get J. D. on the phone and tell him I want the Stamps."

So Elvis's organization sent tapes to us of the songs he would sing and the boys learned the songs and rehearsed until they had all the songs down pat.

Our first date with Elvis was in Minneapolis, and I went along just to see how well the boys did. When we reached Minneapolis and checked into the hotel, we were summoned to the ballroom for rehearsal. That's the way Elvis liked to rehearse, in the hotel, with full sound set up.

Elvis came in and greeted us, calling each member of the quartet by name. When he came to me, he said, "J. D., how're you doing? I'm glad you're here. If I'd known you would have backed me, I would have had you years ago, but I never thought you would."

He stepped up to the mike and we were motioned into places. The Stamps Quartet went to their mikes and I took a seat and reared back to listen. Suddenly, Elvis looked at the quartet and then at me.

"What do you think you're doing, J. D.?" he asked.

"Me? Oh, I'm just going to listen," I said.

"Listen, my foot!" he said. "Get up here. I want you to sing."

"We've got a bass singer," I said. "Richard sings the bass."

"I don't care who's singing," he said, and a smile touched the corners of his mouth. "I want some of those '56 endings." He meant some of the slurs I always tack on a song, running down the scale to bottom out on the lowest note I can and still keep the harmony. He remembered those slurs from my Blackwood Brothers days of 1956.

I didn't know the songs. I hadn't memorized anything, and I didn't know what I was doing. But I do have a good ear, and when the boys hit the harmony behind Elvis, I sang along—with Richard singing, too—and when I thought Elvis wanted a '56 ending, I gave it to him. Every time I dragged bottom on a note, Elvis turned around and grinned.

At the end of the rehearsal, Elvis came to me and said,

"That's the sound I've been looking for. Glad to have you on the show."

Well, that was it. For the next six years, as long as Elvis lived, every time he went on stage, the Stamps Quartet and J. D. Sumner went with him. We did give him the sound he wanted, and he liked it.

We had a few personnel changes along the way. Ed Hill wound up singing baritone for us and became Elvis's announcer, bringing him on stage and at the end of the show saying, "Ladies and gentlemen, Elvis has left the building. Thank you and good night." And we changed tenors a time or two. Dave Roland replaced Donnie. Ed Hill replaced Dave. Ed Wideman took Richard's place, and Larry Strickland replaced Wideman. But Elvis got out of us exactly what he wanted.

Even today people ask me how Elvis got such great sound in his personal appearances. The answer is easy. We covered such a range on the musical scale that he couldn't miss. Kathy Westmoreland hit the double high C, Bill Baize or whoever our tenor was hit the high C, either Elvis or Ed Enoch, or both, hit the C, Richard Sterban or Larry Strickland, whoever was singing bass for our quartet, hit the low C, and I hit the double low C. That's what gave Elvis such a big sound. We covered the range from lowest to highest and gave Elvis exactly what he wanted. When we all came in like that on an ending, covering four full octaves on the scale, Elvis would grin like an idiot. He loved it!

The Stamps Quartet's years with Elvis are well documented in another book I wrote with Bob Terrell, called *ELVIS: His Love for Gospel Music*. So I won't go into more detail here.

I will say that those were the most lucrative years of the Stamps Quartet's lives, and some of the best years of my life. We still sang on the gospel circuit when we weren't traveling with Elvis.

People talk about gospel quartets reaching sinners. The gospel quartet never existed that sang to more people from every cross section of life than the Stamps Quartet sang to during those Elvis years. And we did sing gospel. After we'd been with him two or three years, Elvis gave us a spot on the front of his show and everywhere he went, we sang pure gospel to the crowd during our segment. The people loved it, and so did we.

Elvis's death was a great shock to the nation, actually to the world, and it was certainly the biggest shock the Stamps Quartet ever received. He died in 1977 and we went back on the gospel trail. At the same time we sang—and still do—on a lot of Elvis memorial shows. We have done these shows in various parts of the world. We have been tremendously received in Switzerland and other European countries.

I didn't look on Elvis's death as losing a great job but as losing a fine friend, one of the best friends a man was ever privileged to have. He and I became extremely close during our years together.

Vernon, Elvis's dad, wanted me to handle the funeral. I bade Elvis farewell and went on with my life. Some people refused to let him go and still see him now and then, they say. But they are joshing you. Elvis died. I know. I saw him in the casket, felt his face and hands and hair. It was Elvis, all right, not this and that as some "seers" would have you believe. He died. He is today in the Great Beyond. But his memory remains. And I am rich in memories.

CHAPTER TWENTY-THREE

Water Under the Bridge

At this writing, it has been sixteen years since Elvis died, and a lot of water has passed under my bridge. I sing with the Stamps Quartet again after an eight-year absence of the name. I sang those eight years with the Masters V, a quartet of old-timers, and I never loved singing more. I sang with Jake Hess, Hovie Lister, Rosie Rozell, and James Blackwood until they were all forced to quit the road for one reason or another. James quit in May of 1987 after fifty-three years of rolling along America's roadways, singing the gospel. He still sang, but he sang solo or with his sons, Jimmy and Billy, until three or four years ago when he organized the James Blackwood Quartet and went back on the road more than he had been.

Me? I just keep plugging along.

Let's play catchup for a while. Let me bring you up to date.

My mother died in May of 1987 in Lakeland, Florida, at the age of ninety. I spent the last two weeks of her life with her. People feel sorry for you when you lose your mother, or your daddy. Nobody likes to lose a loved one, but Mama was almost ninety-one and her heart was so bad and she had so much pain she couldn't even eat. Once at the hospital I knelt by her bed and asked God to take her on home so she could be with my daddy. She was a tough old girl. She died sitting on the side of the bed. She lived a full life and had reached the point that she was living on nitro-glycerine pills. She just sat there and suffered with chest pains.

I brought her medicine back to Jake Hess because I saw

190

that some of the medicine she took had the same name I had seen on medication Jake was taking. "Take this to your doctor and check it out," I told Jake. "Maybe you can use it." Jake said his doctor told him if he had taken that medicine, it would have blown his heart right out of his chest. It was that strong.

My mother's medicine bill ran more than three hundred dollars a month. They talked about Elvis being on dope! My mother was the one!

I've never been to a funeral like hers. The church was packed and people stood around the walls and outside. They could not get all the flowers in the church. If it had been Hovie's or Jake's funeral, or somebody's like that, it would have been understandable, but she was just an ordinary woman. A godly woman, yes, but just ordinary—with thousands of friends of her own.

For personal reasons, I didn't let any of my friends know she had died. I didn't want my friends feeling they had to send flowers. She got so many flowers anyway that when the funeral was over I sent flowers to every nursing home in Lakeland.

If there is a heaven—and there is—then that's where my mama is.

Daddy passed on thirty years ago, but the rest of us are still kicking. My brother, Buddy, is seventy-five at this writing (1993). He is a retired Church of God minister. He was also the state overseer for the Church of God in West Virginia. Sister Bernice is seventy-eight. Sister Myrtis is seventy-one. I am the baby of the family at sixty-nine. Some baby!

My granddaughter Kathy, who used to follow me around and call me "Big Daddy," is now twenty-nine. She finished college and is married to Greg Hall. She works for AT&T, the telephone company. She developed a computerized bookkeeping system that has been successful. She and Greg are happily married; they have their own home and a boat. They live in Memphis where my daughter, Frances, Kathy's mom, lives. Frances is married to a fine man, Jim Dunn, who was in charge of United Way in Memphis for a number of years.

Kathy was always proud of her Big Daddy and his singing, and she was proud to tell everybody that I sang with Elvis.

She still calls me Big Daddy.

Kathy and Greg made me a great-granddaddy. Their daughter, Jordan, is four years old. When she was two, we recorded an album called *Peace in the Valley,* and on it was an old song entitled *Roll On, Jordan.* Even today, Jordan thinks that song is about her. She won't allow her mother to play anything but *Roll On, Jordan.* She'll say, "Play my song," and they've worn out two tapes already. Kathy and Greg also have a little boy, Denver, my great-grandson. I don't know where all these new names come from. I was bouncing Denver on my knee and he began acting up. I told him, "Boy, if you don't cut that out, I'm gonna change your name to Albuquerque."

My grandson, Jason Enoch, was born when we sang with Elvis. The only thing I ever asked Elvis for was a TCB necklace for Jason, and Elvis said, "You got it." Elvis gave it to him in Murfreesboro, Tennessee, when Jason was two years old. Elvis told me to put it away and give it to him on his twenty-first birthday, which I'm going to do.

Jason developed an Elvismania. He always went to the airport to see us off when we left to sing with Elvis. Elvis always sent his Jetstar to pick us up, and Jason thought that all airplanes belonged to Elvis. When he looked up and saw a plane, he would point to it and say, "Elvis."

We backed Elvis on his records, and we also cut albums of our own, but Jason wouldn't listen to ours. If I put a Stamps record on the stereo, he would demand, "Elvis! Elvis!"

Jason's mom and dad were divorced after Elvis died. I took Jason on some trips to entertain him, and once in Memphis a man named Klaus Kramer of Germany wanted to interview me about Elvis for German television. I had disbanded the Stamps Quartet by that time. Jason wanted to sit in on the interview, which was all right with Kramer and certainly with me, though I told him he would have to keep quiet.

Kramer asked a lot of questions about Elvis, then said, "Mr. Sumner, in Germany the Stamps Quartet is very popular. Why did you disband it?"

I gave a roundabout answer, skirting the truth. "I thought I wanted to retire from singing," I said. "I had three buses I was leasing to others, and after I had heart surgery the pressure of the quartet was so much I disbanded it."

Under my breath, I said to myself, "There. That ought to take care of it."

But Jason began to shake his head. "I'll tell you why they broke up," he said. "Elvis died and Mama and Daddy got a divorce."

I looked at Jason and then at Kramer and shrugged and said, "The kid's telling the truth," and that ended the interview.

Jason was five then, and a five-year-old doesn't have any more sense than to tell the truth.

Jason was a sharp little boy. After Shirley and Ed divorced, I decided I should spend more time with Jason because his daddy wasn't able to spend much with him and I thought it was good for a man to spend time with a boy.

I lived in a condominium with a pool and clubhouse in my front yard.

One Monday I came home early from the office and called Jason. "Hey, man," I said, "you want to go swimming and shoot some pool?"

"Yeah, Big Daddy," he said.

"Okay, get your swim trunks and come on down."

We swam till dark, then shot pool until I was exhausted.

He had enjoyed the afternoon so much I decided to do it again the next day, so I came home early, called Jason and went through the same routine. We swam again until dark, and shot pool until I was sick of swimming and shooting pool. I had had all I wanted!

On Wednesday, my last day off, I did not want to go swimming, but I had made up my mind I was going to be a daddy to Jason, so when I got home I told Mary I was going to call him.

Mary said, "Honey, you don't need to fool with Jason. You need to rest. You're going to kill yourself. Jason can do something else."

I said, "I am spending some time with Jason."

I called him. "Hey, man," I said, "you wanna go swimming and shoot some more pool?"

"Look, Big Daddy," he said, "I have some other things I want to do. I have friends I want to play with. I can't go swimming with you every day."

When I thought about it, the humor of the situation struck

me. He had been taking time out of his schedule to spend with me, the same as I was doing with him.

Jason gave me a big scare once. Elvis sent his plane to Nashville to take me to Dallas on some business, and I decided since it wasn't a singing engagement and since the pilot and I would be the only ones on the plane that I would take Jason along for the ride.

As soon as we were airborne, I got comfortable and went to sleep. I knew Jason couldn't unlock the door, so he would be all right, but when I woke from my nap he was nowhere to be found. I ran all over the plane looking for him, calling, "Jason? Jason?" I checked the hatch to make sure he hadn't opened it.

Finally, I jerked open the door to the pilot's compartment— and there sat Jason in Milo's lap, flying Elvis's 880.

I said, "If I'd known this, I'd have opened the door and jumped."

Not many little boys got to fly Elvis's airplane.

*   *   *

My voice is still strong. It hasn't deteriorated. Most voices fail as their owners' bodies deteriorate. You can sing as long as you can talk, so long as your health is good. Big Jim Waits was one of my favorite bass singers of years ago, and his voice started breaking up at about the age of fifty-five. When I think back to the time Jim was my age, he had trouble even staying on key. It's all according to your health.

I have always asked God for enough brains for two things: to give me enough sense to stay with my wife till one of us died—He granted that wish—and I asked him to get me off the stage when I reach the point that I can no longer sing. I fully intend to leave the stage at that time. And just in case God gets busy and overlooks that last little item, I have posted several friends around the country: "If I reach the point that I can no longer sing and I'm still on stage trying, I want you to come on stage, take my teeth out, and bust me in the mouth!" Then I want them to tell me, "Get off the stage and get out there in the audience and listen."

*   *   *

At one time, the Blackwood Brothers were the epitome of prestige in the gospel music world, and I was proud to be a member. They and the Statesmen were perhaps the most dignified quartets in the business.

But the Blackwood Brothers began to lose this prestige a few years ago, and I saw it coming long before it arrived.

James and I bought the Stamps Quartet Music Company. We don't have it now; Rex Nelon owns it—and it's a good company. But when we bought it we inherited several thousand song books, and the Blackwood Brothers Quartet became the vehicle through which we intended to sell them.

Singing to live audiences four or five times a week, we went through the audiences selling those old song books, three for a dollar—and our people will buy just about anything a quartet has to sell.

One night we came off the stage in Waycross, Georgia, and the Statesmen followed us on stage. James made a song book pitch, and we were supposed to go through the audience selling song books as the Statesmen started their stand.

I took about three steps, and when I heard Hovie come on with that low, drawn-out yell, I turned away from the audience, put my books back on the table and went backstage. When James came back there, I said to him, "James, you can fire me; you can take it out of my part of the quartet; you can do anything you want—but as God is my witness, I will never go through an audience again selling anything. James, we're low-rating ourselves, selling merchandise like that."

I have kept my word.

Promoters won't allow groups to sell through the audience today. They finally got wise.

If I had been the kingpin in gospel music, we never would have started carrying our records with us on our dates. That's why our records are hard to find in record stores. Why should record stores stock our records when we come to town and sell them cheaper than they can be bought in the stores?

Actually, you can buy some of them cheaper from the quartets than they can be sold wholesale to stores.

We don't have a record market like country music because we destroyed it ourselves.

When I took over the Stamps Quartet in 1965, I told the boys we would never go through the audience selling anything. To me, this was a matter of ethics. Other quartets went on stage and plugged how good their records were, but all I wanted the audience to know was that we had records at our table. I figured if our singing didn't sell records, we didn't deserve to sell any.

So I got a lot of laughs with my record pitches, which usually went something like this:

"Ladies and gentlemen, I am supposed to tell you about our records. Yes, we have records for sale. If you don't believe we've got records, just go out in the lobby and you won't see nothing but records.

"But let me give you a couple of reasons why you should not buy our records. Number one, don't buy our records if you don't have a record player. If you don't have one, you can't use our records.

"The second reason you shouldn't buy our records is because inflation is eating up our country. If you believe that, then while we're still up here on stage, maybe you ought to go by our record table and steal a few records."

Bill Baize used to tell me, "Boss, it's funny, but it's not getting the job done."

That was all right. Nobody was getting the job done, and nobody is getting it done today. We all would be selling more records if we had originally opened up the record store sales instead of the record table sales, but of course that was a throwback to the beginning days of gospel quartet singing.

When James D. Vaughan put the first professional quartet on the road in 1910, he did it to sell his company's song books. That was the sole reason for the quartet's existence, and it worked. His song book sales doubled and tripled.

When song books became a music store item, they were replaced among the quartets by records, and quartets simply sold their own just as they had sold the song books.

There have been attempts made to get our records into record stores, but they've been largely unsuccessful. They'll never be successful as long as quartets continue to market their own.

*   *   *

When I went with the Stamps Quartet, James, Cecil, and I owned the Blackwood Brothers and the Stamps quartets jointly. The Stamps was a sort of nothing quartet, and in the windup James and Cecil were perfectly willing for me to take the Stamps and operate it on my own while they retained operational control of the Blackwood Brothers.

Remember, I bought Cecil out of everything we had joint interest in. I bought his part of the Stamps and two music companies. That left James and me with joint stock in both quartets and the music companies, the Gospel Quartet Music Company and the Stamps Quartet Music Company. I didn't draw any money from my Blackwood Brothers quartet stock and James drew none from his stock in the Stamps, so we traded even up. I gave James my Blackwood Brothers stock for his Stamps stock. That gave me full control of the Stamps Quartet and I was pleased with that; there were other things I wanted to do with the quartet.

James and I then worked out a deal in which we divided our other joint holdings. I gave him the Stamps Quartet Music Company and I kept the Gospel Quartet Music Company. We owned three pieces of real estate. I gave him two pieces that weren't fully paid for, and I took one piece that was paid for. That latter transaction only occurred around 1980. We figured at our ages it was best that we divide our holdings instead of giving our families a chance to fight over them.

I still own the Gospel Quartet Music Company. That's where all my songs are, and a bunch of Wally Varner's and Bill Shaw's, and a lot of Bob Prather's songs. There are some rather valuable copyrights in the Gospel Quartet Music Company.

CHAPTER TWENTY-FOUR

Heart Surgery

I have a physical examination every three months. Once in 1978, the year after Elvis died, when my doctor finished my checkup, he came in where I was dressing and said, "You've had two heart attacks."

"Man," I said, "what are you talking about? I haven't had any heart attacks."

"Lie down," he ordered, "and don't get excited. Believe me, you've got a heart problem. You have had two heart attacks."

As I lay there, with him going over me again, I went back in my mind to some events in the past. Once in Dallas I thought I had indigestion. I had gas in my chest. That was less than a year before this appointment with the doctor, and I was doing shows about Elvis for his fans.

At home, the last thing I did at night was drink chicken broth or something hot, and as I sipped it I would swallow air and get indigestion. I would have chest pains until I burped up the gas.

In Dallas I had a suite with a bedroom upstairs and living room and kitchenette downstairs. I went to the kitchen and drank a Pepsi, swallowing air as I sipped it. In a few minutes I burped the chest pains away.

I told the doctor about that incident.

"You were probably having a light heart attack and didn't know it," he said. "It happens."

He ran some more tests on me and then said, "I'm getting you a room in the hospital."

Next thing I knew, they were preparing me for open heart

198

surgery at the hospital, and if anything in this life will get your attention it's heart surgery.

I made all my plans, got my act together. If you have any doubts about whether you're saved, just in case you aren't, you'll go back to see if you've got all the i's dotted and the t's crossed.

I wrote out my will and did everything I knew to do in preparation to die. Who knows?

Meanwhile, the doctor was also making plans for the surgery.

All of this required a couple of days. The doctor told Mary, "Don't let anybody talk to J. D. on the telephone, and he is to have no visitors. None! I want him to have complete rest and build up his body for this operation."

Three people who learned I was going to have the surgery got through to me. Mary let Rex Humbard through on the phone. He was in Argentina. Rex is a very dear friend, and he talked to me and prayed for me and for the surgeon over the phone.

Marty Robbins and James Sego were the other two to reach me.

When Marty called, Mary let him talk to me.

"You may or may not believe this," he said, "but I am a Christian, and I have admired your singing all my life."

He said, "I have had open heart surgery, and if you'll turn it over to God you won't have any problems. God will take care of you."

What he said made sense to me.

"I'll tell you how you can know if you've turned it over to God," he said. "If you worry about it, you haven't turned it over; so turn it over to God completely and you'll be okay."

That did me more good than any telephone call I could have received. I had never talked to Marty Robbins in my life, and I didn't know he knew I existed.

Then James Sego called. He later died on the operating table during heart surgery. James got through to me on his own. Somehow he talked the hospital into putting him through to my room without anybody's okay, and only James Sego could have done that.

"Hey, Big Man," he said, "this is old James. Sego. How you doing?"

"I'm doing fine, James," I said. "It's good to hear your voice."

"Well, I heard that you gonna be operated on there," he said, "and I wanted to call you up and tell you I'm going to be praying for you." He paused and reconnoitered, and added, "I doubt my praying will do much good, but I'm gonna do it anyway."

"James, I appreciate it," I said.

He talked a while longer and I started laughing at some of the things he said. James Sego was a funny, funny man. I don't know which one did me more good, Marty Robbins or James Sego.

As they rolled me down the hall toward the operating room, after administering the anesthetic, I remember quoting the Twenty-third Psalm: "The Lord is my shepherd; I shall not want. He maketh me to lie down in green pastures: he leadeth me beside the still waters. He restoreth my soul: he leadeth me in the paths of righteousness for his name's sake. Yea, though I walk through the valley of the shadow of death, I will fear no evil: for thou art with me. . . ."

That's where I went to sleep—with the assurance that God would be with me and that everything would be all right.

And it was.

After the surgery, it was three months before I got back on the road. The Stamps kept on singing, and I sat in a chair at home. I walked a little morning and night, and my nerves got really bad. I was so weak that when I went down the three little steps to our bathroom, I would have to stand there and get my breath before I could do anything. It depressed me so that I asked, "How am I ever going to sing again in this condition?" I didn't know, so I asked my doctor and he said, "You're not having any problems except with your nerves. Go back to singing and you'll be able to breathe again."

I went with the Stamps the next week.

I don't remember where we sang the first night I was back, but I do remember there were twelve steps leading to the stage. I ran up those steps and when I started to sing I had no breathing problem whatever. Your nerves can do strange things to you.

Gary Buckles, who sang a lot of tenor for the Stamps during

those Elvis years, died in open heart surgery. He was a young man. He had already had heart surgery, and the doctors had told him he would have to have it again within three years. His veins collected cholesterol. His second open heart surgery was three years to the day from the first, and the reason he died was that they couldn't find veins to do his bypasses. His veins were so knotty and closed up that they couldn't use them.

CHAPTER TWENTY-FIVE

Graduates of the Stamps Quartet

Wherever I go singing these days, someone always asks, "Where is Donnie?" or "What's Tony Brown doing now?"

I keep track of all the guys who sang with the Stamps Quartet. They're scattered all over the country, and the thing I like is that most of them are still doing religious work of some sort.

My nephew, Donnie Sumner, has been preaching and singing. He recently moved to Nashville where he has built a studio and is going to get back in the singing business in a big way. He has great talents in production of recordings and tapes, and he can arrange music with the best in the business.

I never had a son and always wanted one. Donnie was my brother's boy, and he had a terrific talent for music—singing, arranging, playing the piano or 'most any other instrument he wanted to play. Having Donnie in my quartet as a lead singer was one of the great thrills of my life because he is the nearest thing to a son that I could ever have. The years Donnie sang with the Stamps were my happiest years with the quartet, and I don't know but what Ed Enoch, Bill Baize, Donnie Sumner, and I probably had the best quartet of all time.

Donnie's ability not only to sing but also to arrange and to direct made the Stamps Quartet better. We used some of Donnie's material and direction on the last record the Stamps Quartet cut in 1993. Like when you sing, "Jeeesus," Donnie would only have one guy say "Jesus." The other guys would sing "Je-us," and that way we didn't have a bunch of S's coming in there. Donnie was a stinker about things like that—things that made a quartet better.

Ed Enoch, my former son-in-law, is back singing with the Stamps Quartet after an absense of almost ten years. Ed is a fine fellow. Even though he and Shirley couldn't make it as husband and wife, he is still like a son to me. Fact is, I'm expecting that Ed Enoch will carry the Stamps Quartet on after I'm dead and gone, or if I reach the point that I can no longer sing. He's the only man who can do it.

It's already arranged in my will. Ed will have the authority to carry on the Stamps Quartet. I think there should always be a Stamps Quartet.

Elvis once called Ed Enoch the finest singer he had ever heard. He is that. Next time you hear us on tape or in person, listen closely to Ed's singing and see if you don't agree.

Mylon LeFevre is a superstar in contemporary gospel music. He has a fantastic testimony and a great rapport with young people. After Mylon left the Stamps and went into rock, he got into drugs pretty deeply. He told me he had a thousand-dollar-a-day habit. He said he sat several times with a cigarette between his fingers and watched it burn up and never felt it. He was so filled with drugs he just sat there and laughed. When his father, Urias, passed away a few years ago, it really brought a change in Mylon's life. Young people like the contemporary gospel he sings, and if it does them good I'm all for it.

Joe Roper is dead. He retired, but still taught at the Stamps-Baxter School of Music, which Zondervan bought along with the Benson empire. Joe was a great teacher. He went back a long way in quartet music.

Big John Hall still sings the gospel. He is an Assembly of God follower, and I suppose if that denomination has a soloist representing the denomination, John Hall is the man. He sings at all their camp meetings and big gatherings, and his popularity hasn't waned a bit.

Roger McDuff lives in Houston and is part owner of a television station in Florida. He still sings solo sometimes.

Jim Hill left the Stamps Quartet and sang with the Statesmen a while, then quit and went into the shoe business. He has since retired from the company he was with and has gone to work for another shoe company. He is quite an operator.

Terry Blackwood is singing in a solo ministry and doing well.

For a while, Tony Brown played piano on the Elvis Presley Show, and from that he became A&R man for a subsidiary of RCA Victor in Los Angeles. When they moved him to Nashville as A&R man, he discovered the group called *Alabama* and signed them with RCA. Since that time he has moved to MCA Records as an executive vice president.

I don't know why everybody I made something out of is doing better than I am.

A few years ago when I was roasted in Nashville, Richard Sterban, who sang bass for the Stamps and then went with the Oak Ridge Boys, said that I had contributed a lot to teaching him how to sing.

Then Tammy Wynette said, "J. D., we all know that you taught Richard how to sing, and Harold Reid (of the Statler Brothers) how to sing, but I wonder what happened: Richard came here today in an armored car just to protect his jewelry, and you came in a pickup truck. Why can't you remember what you taught Richard?"

Sometimes I wonder myself.

Duke Dumas, who came off an Arkansas farm to play lead guitar for the Stamps, is a sessions man in Nashville today. He is a popular sessions man and he's doing fantastically well.

Tim Baty is married, living in Florida, doing church work, and is no longer singing. I understand he is preaching. Tim was a good boy.

Ed Hill, who sang baritone for the Stamps and was the stage announcer for Elvis, sang with and managed the Singing Americans for a while and then came back to the Stamps Quartet. He is with us today, the finest baritone singer anyone could want and a prince of a fellow.

Jimmy Blackwood is preaching and singing, doing a fine job. Billy Blackwood is like my own son. He has a solo ministry guided toward young people.

Bill Baize, our tenor when we went with Elvis, is pastor of the Bellevue Assembly of God Church in Nashville.

Larry Strickland, who sang bass for the Stamps for some

time, married Naomi Judd, the country music queen, and is living happily ever afterward.

Ed Wideman, a Canadian who sang bass with us, was killed in an automobile accident.

Several of these fellows have gone on to be millionaires. I hired Tony Brown at $125 a week and now he's the third most powerful man in the music industry and is making a base pay of over a half-million a year. Dave Roland, who sang baritone with us, started a group called Dave and Sugar and is a millionaire. Richard Sterban went with the Oak Ridge Boys and became a multimillionaire. It has been one of the highlights of my life, seeing these kids grow up to become so successful—and here I am, still singing for peanuts and driving a pickup truck.

I am proud of all the guys who sang for the Stamps Quartet. They are my boys, and I would do anything on earth for any one of them.

CHAPTER TWENTY-SIX

The Masters V

When Shirley and Ed Enoch separated and got a divorce in 1980, I broke up the Stamps Quartet. I really thought I could stay home and relax and play golf and make my living off my buses.

I had two buses, one for which Elvis gave me $25,000 as a down payment and one the Stamps Quartet already had. I leased both buses to other groups.

I have never had a happy bus driver because I can outdrive any driver I ever had, except Glen Tadlock, who drove for the Stamps Quartet.

Both of my buses were leased to REO Speedwagon, a rock group. When the Stamps broke up, I thought I would see what the bus business was like, so I went along on one of the trips and drove one of my buses. I left Nashville and drove my older bus to Greensboro, North Carolina, and had a friend, Jack Howell, drive the newer bus.

We picked up REO Speedwagon and their crew in Greensboro and drove to Charlotte, spent the night, and then drove on to Orlando, Florida, where REO took four days to prepare for a show in the Tangerine Bowl.

I was making $325 a day for my best bus, the TCB bus that Elvis helped me buy, and $265 a day for the other bus. In addition I drew a hundred dollars a day for driving. Every morning I woke up for four days and looked out the window at those two buses, neither of them moving, and realized I was making $690 a day with my hotel room and food furnished, and I really got to enjoying it. I thought I might retire and stay in this business.

With the Stamps Quartet disbanded, I had nothing to do, nobody to sing to, nobody to sing with, and all I did till I made that trip was play golf and try to beat the boredom.

Lewayne Satterfield came in my office one day and said, "You're not going to be happy not singing." She had handled public relations for the Stamps Quartet.

"Oh, yeah," I said, "I'll be happy."

"What you ought to do," she said, "is pick out some men and sing at least a little. You remember the Masters III—Chet Atkins, Floyd Cramer, and Boots Randolph? They did some concerts together, not a lot, but a few—with phenomenal success."

"Yeah," I said lazily, "I remember them."

"Why don't you get a group of men and do some tours each year," she said, "and call yourselves the Masters Five with a V?"

Just a few days later, Jake Hess came into my office in the Sumar Building in Nashville. I mentioned Lewayne's idea and he liked it. He was on the West Coast doing television.

So Jake and I ran with the ball. Our idea was not to be a full-time quartet, but to do three or four tours a year, enough to keep us in the business and keep us interested.

When Jake asked what personnel I was thinking of, I told him James Blackwood, Hovie Lister, Jake Hess, J. D. Sumner, and Connor Hall. All of us were old-timers.

We telephoned Hovie and put the idea to him. He liked it. But he said, "I couldn't do it unless Rosie is included." He and Rosie Rozell owned the Statesmen, and they could take off long enough to do the tours we had in mind each year.

Jake and I agreed. Connor Hall was in feeble health and might not be physically able to make three or four tours a year. Rosie was an old-timer and a great tenor.

Our next problem would be getting James Blackwood away from the Blackwood Brothers long enough to do the tours. We called him and he agreed on the phone, at least partially. "We'll try it at least one tour and see how it works out," James said. His son, Jimmy, was singing James's part with the Blackwood Brothers at that time, and James was only singing three or four songs a night.

We did a tour, and it was very successful. With Rosie on the tenor, James and Jake alternating on lead and baritone, me on the bass, and Hovie playing the piano, we had a good sound from the start. There weren't any spring chickens among us. We all had been singing about a thousand years apiece, and had often sung together.

By that time, Hovie's bass singer had quit the Statesmen and I had joined them, not as a regular member but just temporarily until Hovie found a bass singer. I had no intention of joining the Statesmen permanently—not that I had anything against them, but if I had wanted to be a member of a full-time quartet, I would have kept the Stamps Quartet together.

Hovie could see the potential of the Masters V, and began to faze out the Statesmen in 1980. It was after that first tour that we finally organized the Masters V without James saying yes. We started out with Jake, Rosie, Hovie, me, and a guy from North Carolina named Richard Coltrane, who is a good singer.

It wasn't long before we talked James into leaving the Blackwood Brothers completely, and then we had the Masters V, the group I had set out to have—without Connor Hall, though. The group I put together was the group that had sung at Elvis's funeral.

Connor would have been perfect for the tenor position in the quartet. No one has ever sung more tenor than Connor Hall, who had the Homeland Harmony Quartet for years. He started singing in Greenville, South Carolina, with the Tremont Avenue Church of God Quartet, which became the Church of God Bible School Quartet, and finally evolved into the Homeland Harmony.

Connor was my first choice. Rosie was much the better tenor at the time, but my idea was to go with nostalgia more than great singing. If I'd been after the best singers, I probably would have picked George Younce to sing the bass, but I wanted personalities instead of great singers. Besides, George was much too ugly. A fantastic bass singer, yes, but if I had his voice with my looks, I could have amounted to something.

The first tour we made was in November of 1980. We sang part-time for two such tours, and then we all got to enjoying it and our adrenaline began to flow. A new desire and zeal to sing was regenerated in all of us, so we just threw caution to the wind and went full time.

We talked it over, and all of us being at the age we were, we hoped we could last five years. Actually, we sang for eight years until the other guys had to drop out for various reasons.

I did a television interview in Pensacola, Florida, and the man interviewing me asked what we were trying to accomplish with the Masters V. I said we weren't trying to accomplish anything, that if the five of us hadn't already accomplished it, then it can't be done in gospel music.

We had fun, we sang the songs we loved to sing, songs about Jesus Christ, the happiest music in the world. We did exactly what we wanted to do.

I don't have a lot of money, but nobody in the world has been blessed in being able to do what he wants to do more than I have—and I've made a living at it.

When I was four years old, so my mother said, people would ask me what I was going to do and I'd say I was going to be a bass singer in a quartet, and that's what I've been. I wouldn't trade places with Arnold Palmer, Jack Nicklaus, Tommy Glavin, or anybody. I wouldn't change places with the President of the United States. God forbid! Or with anybody else.

I've always made a living doing something I would pay to do. If I had the money, I'd pay to sing bass.

A positive attitude isn't only necessary to get us through life in good shape, it is also necessary for a quartet man. I once worked with a man who was negative about everything—the food he ate was always bad, his hotel room was never nice enough, the bus was either too cool or too warm, and nothing else was ever right. There have been times in my life when I have been negative about certain things, but by watching this man and knowing how miserable he was and how hard success was for him to attain, I decided negativism wasn't for me.

We drove all night once from Tampa, Florida, to Atlanta, and got in just in time to sleep a couple of hours before going to sing at a big Baptist Church in Cartersville, Georgia. They wanted us to sing one song at church that morning and then put on a concert that night.

When the phone rang with my wake-up call, I thought, "Why in the name of goodness did we agree to go out and sing one stupid song when I need rest as bad as I do?"

Then the thought hit me: You're being negative. How many people would love to have the opportunity to get up this morning and go to a church and sing even half a song? So I turned that thing around, got up, and started feeling good immediately. I went downstairs, drank some coffee, got myself ready, went to the church, and didn't even pull my old routine of staying on the bus until the last minute. I got out and went inside and started shaking hands with the people and talking with them—and I had one of the best days of my life.

If a person could learn to have a positive attitude about life, a million dollars wouldn't come close to comparing with it. I don't care what happens, if we believe in God Almighty, everything happens for the best. If we could sell ourselves on that one thing, what a difference it would make in all of us.

That's the attitude we maintained in the Masters V. We were positive. We knew we had some age on us. We weren't the spring chickens who sang the gospel back in the 1940s, but we could sing it better than ever.

And we thanked God every day for the opportunity.

CHAPTER TWENTY-SEVEN

Back Home

Singing with the Masters V was fun and exciting. We enjoyed the fellowship and the singing. People loved not only to hear us but to see us. After all, we were the oldest conglomeration of gospel singers ever put together in one quartet, and we had been singing for so many years there was nothing we couldn't sing. All our years in gospel music combined gave us more than two hundred years of experience.

The best thing, possibly, was the fact that we all still had our voices. The years hadn't wrecked any of them. Our blend, timing, and stagemanship came out of each of us and communicated with the crowds. We enjoyed the success.

Somewhere along the way, what started out to be fun—just a couple of tours a year—suddenly became work. We were booked every weekend and traveled more than we had before. We were in such demand that some of our road trips turned into forty-eight-day nightmares, and we sang every night.

We would set it up, sing as hard as we could, tear it down, move to the next town, rest awhile, set it up again. . . . The excitement began to fade.

It didn't fade entirely because of the work. We had five people in the quartet who had managed quartets, who had all been emcees, who had ideas on the way to do business and ideas on the way a program ought to be run.

As the new wore off and we settled down to business, feelings of self-importance surfaced in each of us. I knew I was smarter than the rest. Hovie thought he was, James thought he was, Jake thought he was, and Rosie thought he was. So the very thing that caused us to form began to deteriorate within the Masters V.

We never had any troubles with each other, no bitterness, no hard feelings, but when the new wore off and we all came to our senses and realized we had knuckled down to a pretty tough job again, we began to break apart.

Age, mileage, and infirmities took their toll on the Masters V. We were all in or approaching our fifties and sixties when we formed the quartet, and we knew we couldn't sing forever.

Rosie was the first to drop out. He sang a year or so and suffered a heart attack and stroke. It was touch and go with him for a while, but he pulled through. He was replaced in the quartet by Steve Warren, a tremendously talented man from Houston, Texas. Steve was much younger than the rest of us, but he was so talented he could mimic Rosie or Denver Crumpler or Bill Shaw and if you shut your eyes you couldn't tell the difference. So when we did the old Statesman and Blackwood numbers, he sang them exactly as the tenors had sung them forty years before.

But Steve was at his best being Steve. He didn't have to imitate anyone to sing well. It was just a part of the show.

How we were able to work as much as we did, I don't know. We stayed on the road forty days at a time.

I thrive on the road, but others don't, not at our ages.

James went next. I guess he is the biggest phenomenon ever in gospel music. At this writing he is seventy-four and is still as dynamic and as big of voice as he ever was. But at his age, he had no business working as much as we worked. When you're in a quartet, you've got to work. If the guys are ready to leave, you've got to be on the bus. When you're singing by yourself, it's not nearly as much fun, but you can work when you want to. James decided he wanted to spend more time with his wife, Miriam, and wanted to work as he wished, not as we demanded. So he left the quartet. He worked a killing schedule as a soloist, but that was the pace he wanted. He is his own man.

We tried a couple of lead singers who didn't fit the mold, and then hired Jack Toney, one of the greatest lead singers gospel music has ever known. His work with the Dixie Echoes and the Statesmen was legendary. His voice is magnificent, and he is one of the finest fellows you'll ever meet. He fit right in from day one, both in the sound and in the fellowship.

Jake was next to leave. His health took him off the road. His doctors told him he couldn't stand the mileage. We were traveling too much, and he couldn't keep his diet straight. Jake had undergone two open heart surgeries and two cancer operations, but what got him off the road was his diabetes. He can't keep his sugar down on the road, eating here and yonder. He sang for two years a very sick man, and finally just had to quit.

That's when we brought in Ed Hill, the baritone from the Stamps Quartet of Elvis days, and Ed's great voice filled in nicely.

Steve Warren left for a while and another old pro, Shaun Neilsen, who had sung with the Statesmen, Imperials, and other groups, came with us. Shaun has a beautiful high tenor voice. He was a soloist for the Strategic Air Command Band in the U. S. Air Force.

Hovie was last to go. He decided he would follow his own interests and left in August of 1988. He said he intended to reorganize the Statesmen and sing about three nights a week, and he did. Gospel music is better off with the Statesmen back on the road. There is a hole in the business without them.

The bottom line, I suppose, was this: James's heart will always be with the Blackwood Brothers; Hovie's heart will always be with the Statesmen; and I know my heart will always be with the Stamps Quartet.

My relationship with the Stamps doesn't go back just to 1963 when we bought the Stamps Quartet. It goes a long, long way back—to those Church of God camp meetings in Wimauma, Florida, in the 1940s where Mary and I were married in 1941, and where Frank Stamps stood on the platform belting out *Stand By Me* in his fine bass voice, and without benefit of amplification ten thousand people could hear every word he sang. He inspired me to be a singer. I said, "I want to do that." And the word *Stamps* was burned indelibly into my memory.

Most of the "masters" were then doing their own thing again—but that was nothing new: We always did! James has a singing style, Jake has a style, Hovie has a style, I have a style—and not one of us would change our style for anybody. When Jake was singing lead, we were the Statesmen; when James was singing lead, we were the Blackwood Brothers— so basically we were never anybody but our own individual selves.

With four of the five masters gone from the Masters V, there was suddenly no reason to retain the name of the quartet.

The Stamps Quartet, deactivated in 1980, had been idle except for a few weeks in 1987 when Ed Enoch and Larry Strickland formed a quartet and sang under the Stamps banner. Then they decided to sing contemporary and changed their group's name to Heartland.

I decided that with most of the masters gone, I would take the quartet's present personnel, phase out the name of the Masters V, and revert to the name of J. D. Sumner and the Stamps Quartet.

I hired C. J. Almgren, a piano-playing Swede, to replace Hovie, and he turned out to be a fantastic instrumentalist. Hovie himself says few pianists have ever matched C. J. as an accompanist. Jack Toney and Ed Hill stayed on to sing the lead and baritone, and Steve Warren came back to replace Shaun on the tenor.

The Stamps Quartet reappeared as if by magic at the National Quartet Convention of 1988. We were introduced by the convention emcee as the Masters V.

I stepped to the on-stage mike and said, "Ladies and gentlemen, you welcomed the Masters V," and the audience gave us another hand. I said, "Boys, turn around," and they turned around with their backs to the audience.

"Now, ladies and gentlemen," I said as the guys turned back around, "would you welcome J. D. Sumner and the Stamps Quartet?" and a roar of approval went up from the crowd.

Right then, the Masters V drifted into limbo.

After changing back to the Stamps Quartet, I wanted to recapture that great sound we had in the sixties and seventies, and to do that I had to get Ed Enoch back. During the main years of our success, he was our lead singer, and the lead singer establishes a quartet's sound. By that time, Ed and Larry Strickland had given up on Heartland. Larry had married Naomi Judd and all he needed to do then was stay close to Naomi, very close.

I talked to Ed several times and felt each time that he was a little nearer returning. Then in the spring of 1990 Jack Toney left the group to spend more time at home and Ed came back.

I have always said if God gives a man a talent and he doesn't use it, he'll be miserable. I don't care what it is, but I think especially if he gives you a talent to sing, you must use it. Elvis Presley had a talent and I believe he used his talent for the betterment of mankind. He did a lot for a lot of people. Charlie Daniels is a Christian. He never gives a program but that he says, "I wouldn't be fair to you, I wouldn't be fair to myself, and I wouldn't be fair to my God if I didn't tell you that Jesus Christ is my personal savior." That's all he says, but what an impression he has on people who are lost.

Think what a country artist can do with a gospel song. Dolly Parton is a Christian lady. She sang *He's Alive* on national television and used the Christ Church choir behind her and I've never heard a greater impact to reach the lost. Dolly had to tell the network people where to go, more or less, or she could not have sung that song. But look at the number of people Dolly reached that night. I was watching in my den and I'm not a shouter, but I almost shouted myself. She wasn't singing to the people who attend the sing in Waycross, Georgia, or Bonifay, Florida, because those people have heard that song forever and if they aren't saved by now, they may never be. But Dolly reached masses of unchurched people—and, in my opinion, that's using your talent for the Lord.

I said all that to say this: Ed Enoch spent almost ten years out of the business, not singing gospel music, and he said it was the most miserable ten years he'd ever lived. Why? Because he wasn't using the great talent God gave him.

He is now.

Since he returned to the Stamps Quartet, we have achieved the same sound we had during the last part of the 1960s and through the 1970s.

The only man I ever had in my group who put as much into his singing as Ed Enoch was Donnie Sumner. At the time I had Donnie, Ed, and Bill Baize, I'd put Donnie out front first and he would fight that stage like fighting fire, and right behind him I'd throw Ed in front and he would say, "He's not gonna outsing me," and he would swing with both arms. Then I'd run out Bill Baize and he would try to outdo both of them.

I had competition within the quartet but they still helped one another, each still contributed to the other, but when I gave one of them the ball he tried his best to get it over the goal line.

We made one other change. Steve Warren left the Stamps late in 1993 and I hired Rick Strickland to replace him. Rick is young and has the most exciting tenor voice I've heard come into gospel music since Bill Baize. There seems to be nothing Rick can't do, even to singing the songs that Bill Baize sang, and sometimes he goes beyond that. It looks to me that Rick Strickland is going to be one of the greatest and most versatile tenors who ever came into gospel music, and I don't believe the Stamps Quartet has ever been as excited as we are now.

Rick has that humble attitude that's so badly needed in the entertainment business, the reverse of some other tenors I've had. It shows from the stage. I've had people tell me that when Rick sings they couldn't keep from crying. That's because he sings from his soul. Rick will give us what we need. Every once in a while you need some new blood in a quartet and I think Rick will give us another five or ten years of exciting gospel music—if the Lord lets me live that long.

I would have hired Rick a number of years before I did, but he was the type of man who is very loyal to the people he works for. He sang first with the Singing Americans and then with the Kingdom Heirs, the Dollywood quartet. He had a little bout with cancer but that was cleared up and Rick came to me and said he was ready to join the Stamps Quartet. He said he had always wanted to sing with the Stamps, always wanted to sing with J. D. Sumner. As soon as I found out I could get Rick, I began making arrangements for this to happen.

When George Younce heard I had hired Rick, he told Glen Payne, "Rick Strickland is going to be the next star in gospel music. J. D.'ll make him a star and it won't take him long."

There is such a thing as natural stage presence and Rick's got it. That's what the Statesmen and Blackwood Brothers had for so many years.

The Stamps Quartet stands at a crossroads today. Opportunities are opening up in every direction. We sang on the Grand Ole Opry early in December of 1993, doing both the Friday and Saturday shows and the crowd gave us a standing ovation.

We have been asked to become regular members of the Opry and I'm giving that some thought. It would take up twelve of our best dates of the year, but I'm told it would also bring in more good dates and probably increase the size of our crowds on the road.

At my age, the thought of settling down to sing in one place for at least a part of the year is attractive.

The Elvis people put together a show in Memphis early in 1993, featuring the Memphis Symphony Orchestra and the Stamps Quartet. They took the television special, *Aloha From Hawaii,* and eliminated all the tracks except that of Elvis's voice and projected him on a giant screen on stage and then the Stamps Quartet and the Memphis Symphony backed him. We did about four or five songs that way, and then they used a clip from *Elvis on Tour* in which Elvis stopped the program and said, "Ladies and gentlemen, here's a song that I don't sing on. It features J. D. Sumner and the Stamps Quartet, *Sweet, Sweet Spirit.*" The lights dimmed on Elvis and came up on the Stamps Quartet and we sang the song.

Jack Soden, who manages Graceland, told us after the show, "I was never able to attend an Elvis concert, but when you fellows sang tonight I looked around at those people in the Memphis Symphony in their long gowns and ties and tails and there wasn't a dry eye among them." We finished the program singing with the symphony orchestra. The Memphis Municipal Auditorium was sold out for that performance.

They're talking about taking that show worldwide, using local symphony orchestras. Elvis is dead, but that show was the nearest thing to Elvis being there that we've ever done.

Bob Whitaker, director of Opryland, told me if they didn't want to take it on the road, he'd like to put it on at Opryland as a regular show, playing about eight months out of the year. They're going to give Branson, Missouri, some competition.

The show was really phenomenal. If the show becomes a regular anywhere, the Stamps Quartet's pay would be $7,500 a performance, and if we had a hundred or more days a year like that, I could buy myself some new teeth.

All of this, of course, is speculation, but the Stamps Quartet is recognized all over the U.S.A. and, through the Elvis shows we do, we're now known worldwide.

With or without all of this, I'm completely at home with the Stamps Quartet.

I will never sing with another quartet. From now on, I will be in the Stamps Quartet.

This is it!

J. D. Sumner and the Stamps Quartet! The name has a ring to it that I like.

CHAPTER TWENTY-EIGHT

A Happy Family Life

We always had a happy family life. I love kids and I doted on Frances and Shirley as they grew up. Now the grandchildren and great-grandchildren keep things lively around our house.

When our granddaughter Kathy was six she came over from Memphis to spend a Saturday with Big Daddy. She told her mother and Mary to go somewhere and leave us by ourselves.

I started looking for something to do and asked her how she would like to go play golf. I didn't know how in the world I would entertain her all day, but I thought if I could get her on the golf course, that would be a start.

I told her I had a golf cart that she could ride in, and she said she'd love to play golf.

On the first tee we met Paul Downing and Rex Nelon, a couple of bass singers, who were about to tee off. They waited for us. I got the cart, put Kathy in it, and we started out.

She got a kick out of it for three holes, then she became restless. She was most distracting when one of the other guys was trying to knock in a putt.

After the third hole, Kathy decided she'd played enough golf, so we quit and went home.

Kathy turned on the television set and said she was hungry. I made two peanut butter and jelly sandwiches. I wiped what peanut butter was left on the knife on the top of her sandwich and served her, but she took one look at the sandwich and said she didn't want it, didn't like the way it looked, that the peanut butter was supposed to be inside the sandwich, not outside it.

We went round and round and I wound up making her another sandwich. It's tough to outwit a six-year-old.

She used to ask me for money every time she came to see us, but her mother overheard her one day and threatened mayhem if she asked for any more money.

Next time they came, Kathy didn't ask for money. She strutted up to me and said, "Big Daddy, I don't have any money." So I gave her a dollar and told her mother to leave her alone. "She didn't ask for money," I told Frances. "She just told me she didn't have any and left the decision of what to do about it up to me."

* * *

The Stamps Quartet left Nashville in the middle of the night bound for Texas and hit Memphis soon after daylight. We took a few minutes to swing by Frances's house, and Kathy was getting ready to go to school. She was in kindergarten.

When her school bus came, she decided she didn't want to ride it, that she wanted me to take her in the quartet bus. Of course, she won, and I told the boys to get out and go in the house and drink some coffee, that we needed the bus for a while.

I put Kathy in the front seat and drove her to school. She was the only kid in Memphis that day who rode to school in her own private $150,000 bus, and she enjoyed every turn of the wheel.

We parked in the street in front of the school and Kathy wanted me to go and meet her teachers. She told them I was her Big Daddy and had brought her to school in my school bus.

We wound up taking all the teachers out to look at the bus.

I told her then that I had to go and kissed her and patted her on the bottom and as I turned to leave, she said:

"Big Daddy, you know what? I'm plumb broke."

Cost me a dollar.

CHAPTER TWENTY-NINE

An Understanding Family Helps

Mary and I had been married fifty-one years when she died, and if you were to figure all the time I had been home with my family during that time it wouldn't amount to ten years.

I love gospel music as much as I love my wife and family, and believe me, I do love them. I am dedicated to the cause of gospel music as much, possibly even more, although it sounds pretty harsh to say it, than I am to my family life. If I were not, I would have been home with my family more.

I don't kid myself, never did.

Mary and my daughters understood this and accepted it. They were dedicated to the cause, the same as I was.

I attribute much of my success to Mary. A man came to me at the National Quartet Convention and said, "J. D., you've received many honors, and so have James and Hovie and the others, and they're deserved, but what about your families? What about those who stay behind and suffer, even to the point of sometimes being ignored? What about them? Do they ever get what they deserve? Are they ever recognized?"

To be perfectly honest, they seldom do get what they deserve, but this doesn't keep me from personally recognizing that had it not been for Mary and her willingness to do the things she did for me to stay in the quartet business, certainly I could never have accomplished what I have.

A lot of people have asked me what it takes to be successful at quartet singing. One of the main things, I've always maintained, besides having or developing the talent, is to have a companion who stands by you regardless.

The year 1992 was my fiftieth year of singing gospel music professionally, and there never was a time that Mary did not completely stand by me in my desire to sing, at least not after that time early in our marriage when she threatened to leave if I went singing.

She stood by me through every change I made. When I left the Blackwood Brothers, she and Shirley and Frances were upset, but they still stood squarely behind me in my change to the Stamps Quartet.

So I had fifty years with a wife who had the ingredients necessary for me to conquer the great struggle I had to go through, just as many other singers did. There have been many men who could have been great gospel singers but their wives prevented them from doing so because they didn't stand behind them and support them in every way.

Until the day she died, Mary supported J. D. Sumner in everything I did, every change I made, every decision I made. Without complaint or hesitation she stood behind me when I decided to leave Tampa and join the Sunshine Boys, a move that finally put us in the major leagues of gospel singing.

I attribute at least sixty percent of my success to my wife.

Mary preferred to stay in the background, but she was always there, listening in the audience, giving me the good, critical advice a husband needs, keeping a warm home for me to come home to, and filling it with love and devotion.

She would go to a concert or some place where I was appearing and you'd never know she was there. She never interfered with the work I had to do. I've always had rules in the Stamps Quartet that when a singer's wife comes to a concert, the singer has to do his job at the expense of sitting with her and petting her. He cannot baby his wife and do his job, too, and Mary always respected that rule. She loved to come to the concerts, but she stayed out of the way, always in the background, never tried to get in the limelight, but was always there if I needed her. When the program was over and everything was wrapped up, that's when Mary showed up.

I can't think of a single incident in the fifty-one years Mary and I were together in which Mary did anything to hinder or to slow down my progress as a gospel singer. I can't think of one incident in which she did my career any harm. Everything she did was to help me.

I'm a hard-driving man. I work hard. I am six feet, five and one-half inches tall, and sometimes things would build up inside me until I thought I couldn't go on. Many times I broke down and cried to release the tension, and it was Mary's love and companionship through these times that really gave me encouragement. I knew I wasn't working for myself, but for my family.

Mary was always afraid I was going to have a nervous breakdown.

A boy named Les Roberson, who replaced Jake Hess with the Statesmen a few years ago, was singing out of his range and had some serious throat trouble. He lost his voice.

Mary and Shirley were concerned about the same thing happening to me, and I said, half joking and half serious: "If it did, I'd be able to stay home more."

Mary cringed. "No, honey, that's not what we want," she said. "I know how much you love to sing, and that's what I want you to do. Regardless of how much I want you to stay home, I know that without singing, you wouldn't be you. You wouldn't be the same J. D."

I went to Shirley privately to see how she felt.

"No, Daddy," she said. "As much as we want you at home, we want you to sing. All we want is for you to slow down, be careful, and not wear yourself out."

I didn't consult my other daughter, Frances. She wasn't at home. She was already married and living in Memphis.

I am thankful that my family is dedicated to what I believe in just as much as I am. They are willing to sacrifice for me to do what I believe in doing, to use the talent God gave me.

I was always a fortunate man in that respect.

CHAPTER THIRTY

Homegoing

I didn't even know Mary was sick until I found out she had terminal cancer. I believe she knew a long time ago that something was desperately wrong. She must have been a much stronger person than I had thought. I had always secretly prayed for God to take my wife first so I could see that she was put away and at rest. I did that because I thought she was a weaker person than I am, and I didn't think she could handle my going first. Now, looking back, I believe the opposite: I believe she was much stronger than I am.

One thing I was very weak on was not being able to sit down face to face with her and discuss that she had cancer and was going to die. Even after we took her home from the hospital, after the doctors told us there was nothing they could do to save her life, that they could only prolong her agony, she never discussed this with me, never brought up the fact that she was going to die. She seemed to be trying to protect me and I was trying to protect her, and all along the bottom line was that she must have known she was dying.

Since I was gone singing a lot of the time—at Mary's insistence—I asked our daughters, Shirley and Frances, and our good friend, Nancy Carswell, to help me piece together this story of Mary's last weeks.

Friday afternoon, August 28, 1992, Shirley telephoned Mary from her car. On her way back to Nashville from a business trip, Shirley had not been able to reach either Mary or Jason to let them know she was coming. She thought it strange that she didn't find Mary in the office because Mary rarely went home before 3:30 or 4:00 in the afternoon, and Shirley had called the office off and on all morning.

Then when Shirley dialed our home, Mary answered and said she'd had one of her headaches all day and had left the office early. Shirley told her that she would be home soon and would call later.

On Saturday, Mary would always go to the beauty shop, do her grocery shopping, and get things ready for me to come back to town off our weekly singing tour. She usually drove by Shirley's house and dropped off something she had bought for Jason, but mostly she would just stop long enough to deposit the goodies in the usual hiding place and wouldn't actually see Shirley and Jason. He especially liked Pepsi, and Mary kept him well stocked. Shirley had a lot to do that Saturday and didn't think anything about not talking to her mother that day.

Mary usually called Shirley early on Sunday. Both were early risers. When she called that Sunday morning she sounded like Shirley had never heard her before. Her voice was small, frail, almost childlike, and she seemed to have trouble talking. As soon as Shirley heard her, she knew something was wrong. Mary said her head had been "splitting" since Friday and she had had nothing to eat. Suddenly Shirley was frightened out of her wits: This was not like any other time Mary had had one of her headaches.

Just as Shirley jumped into her jeans and headed for the door, I called her. I had just telephoned Mary and knew she was in trouble. I told Shirley I had just talked to Mother and for her to get over there as quickly as she could because something was wrong. The guys on the bus had been talking that weekend about things Mary had said and done recently that didn't add up, and I was really concerned about her. We weren't getting home to Nashville till Tuesday morning.

Shirley stopped and bought some of Mary's favorite foods and drove on to our house. As she tried to encourage her mother to eat, Shirley watched Mary stare into space as if she were trying to remember what she wanted to say but couldn't get the words right.

Shirley remembered back a few weeks when I collapsed on stage in Memphis at an Elvis reunion concert. My heart had acted up and I simply blacked out. They put me in the hospital for tests, and Shirley, who was at the concert, telephoned Mary the next day to come to Memphis. But Mary seemed withdrawn and hadn't really liked the idea of driving herself to Memphis, which she had done many times.

Looking back, Shirley believes that Mary could not face the responsibility of driving that day and was frightened at the prospects.

Anyway, Shirley took Mary to our doctor and he examined her and ran a couple of tests and told Shirley there was nothing to worry about, that Mary only had what is called Trans Global Amnesia. He said it made her forget and become confused, but that it only lasted a short time and she probably wouldn't have it again.

But by the time Shirley got Mary to the car, Mary had to have help walking and getting in her seat. Mary wouldn't let Shirley spend the night with her, but made her go on home and care for Jason. Before she went to bed, Mary telephoned a neighbor couple and asked if they would come over in the night if she needed them. She said she had fallen several times recently but hadn't hurt herself.

Shirley met me when the bus got in the next morning and we drove straight home. The house keys were lying on a table on the patio, and we both knew something was wrong. Mary had left the keys there in case she couldn't answer the door— and she couldn't. She was slumped in a chair, leaning to the right as if she had fallen in that position. When we got to her she said she couldn't move her right arm. Her arm was paralyzed, and though we didn't realize it at the time, her motor skills were beginning to falter. That's why her walking was getting slower and slower.

I called the doctor and immediately took Mary to St. Thomas Hospital for tests. The doctor gave me some paperwork and told me he had scheduled an MRI for that afternoon. We put Mary in the car and I gave the papers to Shirley in the back seat, and when she saw what the doctor had written she thought she would faint. The orders read, "Rule out brain tumor."

Shirley said she knew at that moment that Mary was going to die. She had finally fit all the pieces together of things that had been happening to Mary for weeks.

"I never had such a hopeless feeling in my life," Shirley said.

The doctor was supposed to call me early the next morning with the results of the MRI, but Shirley had to go to her office for a few minutes and called the doctor first and asked him not to call me before she returned at nine. Because of my heart condition, she didn't want the doctor to break the news to me when I was alone. And Shirley knew what the news would be. She really had figured it out.

The phone rang just after Shirley got back, and the doctor broke it to me quickly. He said, "Mary has three massive brain tumors that are melanoma and has but one to three months to live." He said the cancer had not started in her brain but had begun elsewhere in her body.

About that time Jim and Nancy Carswell, very close friends of ours from Hendersonville, North Carolina, arrived to spend a few days with Mary and me, and I was glad to see them, but they were stunned at the news. We called Frances in Memphis and she came as soon as she could.

Seventeen years earlier, Mary had a melanoma mole removed from her arm, and I have heard that melanoma will show up again somewhere else; so for all reason in my mind I believe that's where it came from. I think the cancer had been dormant in her body for seventeen years and suddenly came to life.

The doctor said the cancer was all over her body—in her bones, in her breasts, in her kidneys. She was literally eaten up with cancer.

After conferring with our doctor and a cancer specialist, I learned that the procedure would be to give her chemotherapy for the brain cancer, but they said there was nothing they could do about the bone cancer.

They said they might be able to prolong her life as much as a year, but that the bone cancer produced the most excruciating pain there was, and there was little or nothing they could do to control the pain.

The doctor had told Mary in the hospital that she had tumors on the brain and she told him she didn't want radiation and didn't want anyone to cut on her. So the girls, Frances and Shirley, and I opted not to give her chemotherapy because it would have been ten weeks of torment and all of her hair would have come out.

Mary was always a very proud, dignified, and classy lady. You never saw her in public when she wasn't dressed to the ultimate. She was the kind of woman you could take anywhere you wanted and be proud.

She always wore high heels, always dressed like she was going to church, because she knew I liked her dressed up. Once when I was singing in California, Mary went to see Becky Simmons at Century II Promotions. Becky said, "Mary, why in the world are you wearing high heels today?"

"J. D. likes for me to wear them," Mary said.

"But J. D.'s in California," Becky returned.

"I don't care," Mary said. "He likes for me to wear them."

That was Mary, loyal, true, and classy.

To my knowledge when Mary passed away she weighed within two or three pounds of what she did when we got married. She was a very trim woman.

I kidded her a lot and referred to her in our act on stage, about how trim she was. I told the audience at the Grand Ole Gospel Reunion in Greenville, South Carolina, that Mary was sitting on the front row.

"Stand up, Honey," I said.

She stood up and gave the crowd a small wave of her hand.

"Ain't she something?" I said. "She's got the body of a twenty-two-year-old woman—and I can't do nothing about it but cry a lot."

Three years before Mary passed away, we met Jim and Nancy Carswell. I've never seen Mary take to anybody as fast as she took to Nancy. She just more or less adopted Nancy as her third daughter. Up until Mary's illness, they telephoned each other once or twice a week, and the Carswells came to all of the appearances of the Stamps Quartet that they could manage, especially if Mary was going to be there.

Nancy came to Nashville when Mary became ill and stayed with her through the entire sickness.

When Mary was in the hospital, Nancy went down to the gift shop to find her a gift and bought a small guardian angel pin. She pinned it on Mary's gown and told her that she now had her own guardian angel to look after her. Shirley came to Nancy later and said she needed a guardian angel, so Nancy went back to the shop and bought pins for Shirley, Frances, Kathy, and herself. That was the beginning of Mary's guardian angel caretakers.

When we brought Mary home to stay, Nancy stayed with us to the end. Shirley and Frances stayed with her, too, every minute they could. My brother R.H.'s wife, Nell, spent about half or three-fourths of that time with us. And Sally Enoch, Ed's mother, was there a lot. So was Becky Hughes. There were usually four or five women, all of whom Mary loved very much, taking care of her. One week a niece of ours, Sharon, in whom Mary had a lot of confidence, spent several days with Mary and had planned to spend much more time with her had Mary lived. So there was no lack of loving help.

With that many people around constantly, you'd have thought they would get in each other's way, but they didn't. Each had her job to do, and Mary was the one who delegated the work.

Frances took special note of the way Mary organized things, even though she was desperately ill. She apparently felt that everyone around her should be made to feel useful.

I put her robe on her, very gently pulling it over her paralyzed arm, and from that time on I was the one to handle the robe. Shirley's job was to place Mary's immobile arm on a pillow, putting it just so, and Shirley also became master of placing the pillows behind Mary's head and back. "Shirley knows just how to do it," Mary would say.

Nell and Sally handled most of the cooking and also became prayer warriors, often leading all of the girls out loud in prayer, and they counseled with all of us.

Nancy prepared cool washcloths for Mary's head, and once she started that, Mary didn't think anybody could cool her head as well as Nancy. Everybody called Nancy the "Ice Lady" because she was forever crushing ice for Mary until someone suggested that we buy ice already crushed. Becky Hughes became the expert in administering therapeutic massage. If anyone tried to rub Mary in Becky's absence, Mary would say, "Wait for Becky. She knows exactly how to do it."

Mary even asked the girls to call Shirley and Frances's cousin, Sharon, and ask her what she had rubbed on my mother's neck during her last illness, and Sharon would come and handle that.

Frances kept up with Mary's medicine, and even though there was good backup help available for that task, Mary always expected it of Frances.

One evening Nancy was reading a first edition copy of my book, *Gospel Music Is My Life*, which is incorporated in the book you are now reading, and as she read the part about Frances coming to live with Mary and me, she began to laugh.

Mary was awake. "What's so funny?" she asked.

"I'm reading this part about you and J. D. adopting Frances," said Nancy, "and about how silent she was until she began to sing *Pistol-Packin' Mama.*"

Mary began to laugh also, remembering the incident. Frances and Shirley came into the room to see what the giggling was about, and when Nancy told them, they began to laugh, and Frances suddenly started singing *Pistol-Packin' Mama.* Shirley and Nancy joined in the singing, and Mary looked at them as if they had lost their minds.

They probably did look pretty ridiculous, standing around the bed singing *Pistol-Packin' Mama.*

When their performance ended, Mary smiled and said, "You're all crazy." But the girls could tell that she had enjoyed the song.

As time went on, Nancy would bring up other incidents from the book and Mary loved to talk about them. Today, Nancy cherishes those moments she spent in that manner with Mary.

An item of amazement to all the Guardian Angels were the scrapbooks Mary kept on my career. She had every clipping, every picture, every award, every relic, everything that had anything to do with my singing from the time I was with the quartets in Florida on up through the Sunshine Boys, the Blackwood Brothers, and the Stamps Quartet. I don't know of another wife in gospel music who has done that for her husband's career—especially for fifty years as Mary did it. She truly was a dedicated wife and mother who appreciated and was proud of all of the accomplishments I have made in a half-century of singing. Her scrapbooks are priceless to our family.

In the earlier weeks of Mary's illness, Frances's daughter, Kathy, and son-in-law, Greg Hall, decided to bring their three-year-old daughter, Jordan, to see Mary. They had debated whether to bring her or not, thinking Jordan might disturb Mary. But they brought her on, and Jordan, who was our only great-grandchild at the time, sat in the floor, coloring, and the whole time she was there she was quiet as a church mouse, almost as if she sensed the seriousness of the situation. We often saw Mary's eyes watching Jordan, and at one point Jordan wanted to get on a chair so she could see Nana better.

One day Mary began quoting Acts 3:6, "Silver and gold have I none, but such as I have, give I thee: In the name of Jesus Christ of Nazareth, rise up and walk." We knew then that she would receive her ultimate healing in heaven if she didn't receive it here.

Mary said more than once that she sensed the many prayers, which was most apparent in the presence of peace and the absence of fear.

Several weeks into her illness, Mary said, "I'm going home in the morning," and when we assured her that she was already home with her family and friends, she said again, "I'm going home in the morning." It became obvious that she was referring to her final home with Jesus.

And she comforted us. To Frances, Shirley, and me three days before her death, she said, "Calm down. All is well." We knew then that her storm was already past.

A day later, she showed her true colors. Suddenly she perked up and said, "Bye, y'all; I've had a good time."

It is only natural to look back on those last few weeks and recognize the trial she was going through, but the inspiration she was to all of us told us that without question she was a courageous woman of great character who knew Christ personally.

I can't say enough for Alive Hospice. When a patient is taken home to die, when there is no hope remaining, Hospice will send out a registered nurse three times a week, and on the other days will send nurses who bathe the patient and see that she is comfortable. These are evermore dedicated people. We talk about having a ministry in gospel music. These people have a ministry! It's the most wonderful organization in the world—Alive Hospice. I hope there's one in every town.

Near the end, Mary would say that Jesus was going to come and get her and she was going to be with Jesus. She would say, "Ain't God good? Praise God!"

As she was passing away, she was alert and very much aware of what was going on. I was not at the house, but they all told me about her going.

The last day that Mary lived, Hospice sent out a woman who was studying to be a missionary, and while Mary was passing away, they all stood around the bed and this lady prayed, and it became almost a praise service, almost like rejoicing, they were praising the Lord so well.

Ed Enoch, Shirley's former husband, was there. Mary's passing seemed to solve the problems Ed and Shirley had between them. Theirs was a rather bitter divorce and this really healed the wounds because they were all standing at the bed praising the Lord. Sometimes divorce causes really bad wounds and scars, but all of them are now healed between Ed and Shirley, and I thank God for that for the benefit of their son, Jason. If any great thing came out of this tragedy, it was the healing of their wounds.

I don't condemn anybody for divorce. I didn't condemn Shirley or Ed, and neither did Mary. I believe that some people weren't meant to be together, and it happens that J. D. Sumner and Mary *were* meant to be together. We were for fifty-one wonderful years.

Ed is still a member of the Stamps Quartet—and Mary is the reason Ed came back to the quartet. When Jack Toney left, Mary called Ed and asked him to come back. She told him I needed him, which I did, and Ed believed Mary.

Mary always loved Ed. In the hospital, when he came into her room, she would say to the nurses, "That's my son-in-law." Ed also loved Mary very much.

Her passing was a very, very spiritual one, just unbelievable. Ed sang the complete song, *Victory in Jesus*, at Mary's bedside. He sang it *a cappella*. They told me that when Ed was singing Mary opened her dark brown eyes and they were clear, and she tried to smile.

What a way to go!

She died October 20, 1992, at about eight o'clock. We had the wake the next night at Woodlawn Funeral Home, and the funeral was the next day, October 22.

To preach the funeral we were fortunate to get Brother Harold Hunter, Mary's favorite preacher. He is a good friend of ours. I remember once during Mary's illness when Brother

Hunter telephoned that he was coming to see Mary, she perked up and made the girls clean up the house and get it looking right. And then she put a flower in her hair.

Brother L. H. Hardwick, pastor of Christ Church in Nashville, and my brother, Reverend R. H. Sumner, also agreed to take part in the service.

On the night of the 21st, the Crook and Chase television show ran a three-and-a-half minute memorial to Mary on The Nashville Network. I thought it was extremely nice for a network show to take that much time to remember her, and I will always appreciate that.

The Cathedrals were in town, and George Younce called me on the 21st to offer his sympathy. I asked if they were going to be in town the next day, and he said, "Yes, but we're making pictures tomorrow morning and playing Owensboro, Kentucky, tomorrow night."

"You think there's any way you fellows can sing at Mary's funeral?" I asked.

"I don't know," he said. "Let me talk to Glen and if there's any way we can possibly do it, we will."

The funeral was at 11:30 in the morning, and I thought they might be able to work it out.

George called back in a few minutes and said they would be glad to sing or do anything they could. I'll never forget that. They had to scramble to do it, I know, but George Younce and Glen Payne and the other guys in the Cathedral Quartet are some of the best friends I've got in the business.

Mary didn't like what she called "funeral songs." At our recording sessions, when she had a chance to sit in and listen, she would say to me, "I hope you don't record too many of those funeral songs."

Because of that we didn't approach her funeral in the manner of most.

George Younce sang *I'm a Child of the King*, and Glen sang *Jesus Face to Face*, neither of which was a funeral song.

We set up the Stamps Quartet's P.A. system in the funeral chapel and I told Steve Warren, "Cut it wide open." Steve grinned and opened it up. I then told George Younce, "When you get out there I want you to sing as loud as you can. I want you to try to wake Mary up. And don't stand behind the casket like most people do; come out there and stand beside it. But remember, you old goat, if you do wake her up, she's gonna come up from there and kick your butt because you can't sing as good as I can."

George and I have always cared for each other; there's nobody I love more than George Younce. No matter how ugly he gets in his old age.

I got Bill Baize, Ed Enoch, Donnie Sumner, and Larry Strickland to be an old-time Stamps Quartet. Mary used to love to hear them sing in harmony. Standing beside the casket they sang *I Can Feel the Touch of His Hand* and *You'll Never Walk Alone.* They didn't sing like they were at a funeral, but like they were at an All-Night Singing. If you've never heard Bill Baize sing *You'll Never Walk Alone,* you've missed something.

Then the present Stamps Quartet sang with George taking my place. They sang *God Shall Wipe Away All Tears.* Donnie Sumner sang a solo, *Take Your Burdens to the Lord and Leave Them There,* and a song that his wife, Marti, wrote, *Till It All Shall Pass.*

Ed Enoch again sang *Victory in Jesus* without accompaniment.

I've never been to a service that was more spiritual than that. We're told in the Bible by Paul, "To be absent from the body is to be in the presence of the Lord," and "For me to live is Christ and to die is gain." We are really tested at a time like this, like losing one so close as your wife, and the Scripture is all we have to hold on to. My wife is in a better place, at home with Jesus, just like she said she was going to be. That's where all true Christians are going to wind up, at home with Jesus. The final resting place is with the Lord, and I feel just as sure as my name is J. D. Sumner that my wife is in the arms of Jesus today, and I will see her again.

Mary's body was placed in a crypt in a mausoleum in Woodlawn Cemetery in Nashville. The cemetery is owned by Woodlawn Funeral Service. When Mary's service was over, all they had to do was take her down the hall and put her in a real quiet room that was set aside for us. She's resting there. That's where I will be laid to rest.

So I dedicate this entire book to the memory of my loving wife, Mary Agnes Sumner, because without her there wouldn't have been a book. Without her, there probably would not have been a lifelong gospel singer by the name of J. D. Sumner.

She was an understanding wife, a dedicated and loyal wife, and she was the glue that held our marriage together. Being perfectly honest, there were times in the fifty-one years of our marriage that the marriage became fragile on my part, and the glue that bound us together was Mary.

The one thing I can promise now is that I am a Christian, and, Mary, our marriage will be final.

CHAPTER THIRTY-ONE

On the Road Again

I realize I'm stealing a line from Willie Nelson in the title of this chapter, but that's where I am now—on the road again. There is no way I can tell you how much I love my family, but without Mary at home, it isn't home anymore. The Stamps Quartet is now an even bigger part of my life than it was before, and being a person who has always loved to be on the road, we'll stay on the road and sing just as much as the other guys can stand it.

Their situations are different, I realize, but there isn't a man in the quartet who doesn't love to sing. Before Mary died, the Stamps Quartet traveled more than any other group in gospel music, and I know that all the guys like to be on the road. So without interfering with their family life, we'll travel just as much as they want to.

To us, traveling isn't just singing. It has become a way of life. We are comfortable on the bus, comfortable in any auditorium or shopping mall, or, for that matter, in any church. We do not intend to sing just the gospel from here on out. We'll sing gospel songs and continue to do gospel concerts, but we'll also sing those great ballads of America, and some of the good, inspirational country songs, and certainly the love songs that we so loved to sing while standing just behind Elvis.

The Stamps Quartet today is the most versatile quartet in the world. We sing all those styles with equal ease, and we can switch from gospel tonight to Western ballads tomorrow night and good old Americana songs the following night, and sing all of them with equal aplomb.

A song is a song. I'm not saying there are no bad songs—

236

I've heard the words of some I wouldn't even listen to again, let alone sing. But the songs the Stamps Quartet sings on any of its shows can be enjoyed by anyone in the world, regardless of age, standing, nationality, or tongue.

We go to Switzerland and Germany and other European countries on occasion and sing the songs of Elvis, and we draw tremendous response. We go to Long Beach or Winston-Salem and sing the gospel and we are tremendously received.

That's the way it should be. Music is the universal language—not gospel music or rock or country. Just music. I once heard of a man surrounded by savage headhunters who tried to talk to them and, of course, wasn't understood. Then he began to croon soothing songs and before long the headhunters lowered their weapons, canted their heads, and began to smile and then to dance, and the man walked away unharmed.

Music has been my life. There was a lot of music between Mary and me. Music fills my every bone, and all of my waking hours.

Yes, sir, I'll bounce my great-grandchildren on my knee—my grandchildren are too big for that—but while I'm doing it I'll sing them a little song.

Then I'll go on stage that night and sing a song for you. You can bet that when you see old J. D. Sumner and the Stamps Quartet coming, you'll be able to hear the music.

And when I'm gone, I hope you can still hear it.